Praise

'Lee has created a book to break down the information you need for all things martial arts. It's a tool for good fighters that want to learn how they can use their skill set to make a great living, while still keeping their integrity and helping many people through the world of martial arts.'
— **Michael Venom Page 'MVP'**, multiple-time kickboxing world champion, Bellator World Champion contender

'Lee has taken all of his knowledge and experience and put it into these pages. He is now blessing all of us with this knowledge and paying it forward. I hope you all enjoy this book like I did; it is a masterful guide and I can't wait to read it again.'
— **Raymond Daniels**, Bellator World Champion

'Lee has built one of the biggest martial arts organisations in the UK, and what he has put together in this book will help all instructors from any styles if they want to learn how to make a living doing what they love.'
— **Braulio Estima**, Multiple BJJ world Champion and ADCC World Champion and hall of famer

'What has been set out in this book sums up everything you need to do to attain a strong mind and dominate in your arena of martial arts. It also explains how to be the very best at what you do and use your skills to help others, while building and scaling up a successful business.'
— **Mark 'Billy' Billingham MBE**, of Channel 4's 'SAS Who Dares Wins', former Regimental Sergeant Major of 22 SAS

'In this book, Lee shares the experiences that have made him the way he is: elite. He also goes over training, coaching and business strategies that have helped me get to the very top. If you're content with being average and mediocre, this book isn't for you. But if you're serious about being the best at what you do, I suggest you start reading.'
— **Elijah Everill**, fourteen-time WAKO World Champion

'This book is the answer to have an insight into the mind of a truly successful human. For anyone who wants to be a better person or create the best martial arts school you must read Elite Martial Arts Instructor.'
— **Drew Neal**, three-time WAKO World Champion, two-time WAKO European Champion and trainer of celebrities

'I highly recommend *Elite Martial Arts Instructor* as an essential resource for understanding and developing a successful MA business model.

This book offers valuable insights and practical tools that can significantly enhance your strategic thinking and decision-making processes. *Elite Martial Arts Instructor* presents a comprehensive framework that enables you to visualise, analyse and understand an innovative business model. Moreover, the book emphasises the importance of continuous iteration and adaptation. Lee explains that business models are not static but evolve over time. I highly encourage you to delve into this book and explore the powerful practical concepts it offers. Prepare to be inspired, challenged and equipped with practical tools that can transform your approach to your MA school. Enjoy the journey!'
— **Roy Baker**, World President of WAKO

'This book was both educating and inspiring. This is a go-to for anyone wanting to up-skill their business IQ and understand the fundamental rules for success across a multitude of industries. For martial artists wanting to pursue a career in the industry, this book is for you.'
— **Damon Sansum**, World Kickboxing Champion, ten-year member of the TKD GB Olympic team

'This book is a collection of knowledge on martial arts and business and would be extremely beneficial to anyone wanting to move up the ladder of success.'
— **Richie Woodhall**, former WBC World Boxing Champion, boxing presenter for the BBC

'*Elite Martial Arts Instructor* is an inspiring book. You will come away with a newfound appreciation for the power of mindset and the role it plays in achieving success. Whether you are a seasoned entrepreneur or just starting out on your journey, the lessons in this book will inspire you to take action and pursue your dreams with a champion's mindset.'
— **Mike Chadwick**, coach, entrepreneur and author, paratrooper and military physical training instructor

'Lee Matthews and this book epitomises the qualities needed to succeed at the very top level in both fighting and business.'
— **Matt Winsper**, two-time World Champion, Karate and Kickboxing

LEE MATTHEWS

ELITE

MARTIAL ARTS INSTRUCTOR

A MILITARY APPROACH TO OPENING, OPERATING AND SCALING A THRIVING MARTIAL ARTS BUSINESS

Rethink

First published in Great Britain in 2023 by Rethink Press (www.rethinkpress.com)

© Copyright Lee Matthews

All rights reserved. No part of this publication may be reproduced, stored in or introduced into a retrieval system, or transmitted, in any form, or by any means (electronic, mechanical, photocopying, recording or otherwise) without the prior written permission of the publisher.

The right of Lee Matthews to be identified as the author of this work has been asserted by him in accordance with the Copyright, Designs and Patents Act 1988.

This book is sold subject to the condition that it shall not, by way of trade or otherwise, be lent, resold, hired out, or otherwise circulated without the publisher's prior consent in any form of binding or cover other than that in which it is published and without a similar condition including this condition being imposed on the subsequent purchaser.

I would like to dedicate this book to my wife and three kids. They sometimes miss out on me while I'm helping others, but everything I do is for them.

Contents

Introduction	1
PART ONE Make It Grow	**9**
The Evolution Of The Martial Arts Industry	11
Limiting beliefs and mindset	14
The 4S's	17
Know your value	19
Multiple schools in one area	21
Summary	23
Round 1: Ready (Red On)	**25**
Your business plan	28
Your mission statement	29
Your financial plan	30
The white belt mindset	31
How to prioritise	34
Preparing to launch a school	38

Embrace the chaos	46
Summary	49
Round 2: Relaunch (Green On 'Go')	**51**
Beware negativity	56
Balance versus counterbalance	61
Executing on a plan	64
H-hour: The launch event	65
My martial arts and teaching journey	72
Summary	81
PART TWO Make It Great	**83**
Round 3: Rapid Growth (Advance To Battle)	**85**
My fighting experience and how I raised my game	87
Hierarchy of values	89
Take advantage of laziness	91
Good problems and bad problems	93
External marketing	94
Free face-to-face marketing	103
Internal marketing	106
Change your mindset and the world changes with it	111
Summary	115

Round 4: Retention (The Battle) — **117**
    The small things matter — 120
    Statistics — 122
    Dojo management — 124
    Syllabus and grading — 135
    Competition — 137
    Income stream generators — 142
    Mentoring — 145
    Summary — 151

PART THREE Make A Difference — **153**

Round 5: Restructure (Reorg) — **155**
    Military structures — 158
    Improvise, adapt and overcome — 162
    Growth structure — 166
    Business structures — 173
    Negotiating — 178
    Building a community — 182
    How team TopTen began — 186
    Summary — 191

Round 6: Repeat (Training And Selection) — **193**
    Day 1 – Wednesday — 195
    Day 2 – Thursday — 197
    Day 3 – Friday morning — 198

Day 4 – Monday	198
Day 5 – Tuesday	198
Training future instructors	201
Teamwork and leadership	205
Red flags	207
The 'click your fingers' test	211
Modelling success	213
Summary	223
Conclusion	**225**
Further Reading	**237**
Acknowledgements	**239**
The Author	**247**

Introduction

You have turned your passion for martial arts into a business, but it's not yet as successful as you know it can be. Perhaps you're still fitting it around your day job, getting burnt out and losing your enthusiasm. Or your martial arts business might still be just a dream, and you have no idea how to start.

Whatever your circumstances, it's likely that you know much more about your chosen discipline than you know about business. If this sounds like you, you're not alone. The majority of martial arts instructors are in a similar situation. They are not able to take their business to the next level, so they stay in a cycle of mediocrity because of their love of their discipline, the rewards they get from teaching and their dedication to their students.

What if I told you there was another way? A way you can attract and keep more students and not only maintain your integrity but improve the standard of your students, black belts, instructors and fighters. You don't need to reinvent the wheel. My team and I have created the processes that will help you scale up your business.

I served for eight years in the British Army's elite Parachute Regiment and became an army physical training instructor (PTI). I've competed in martial arts from the age of eight and have been the British, European, and world kickboxing champion multiple times, in various organisations. Over the last twenty-five years, my team and I have built up the UK's biggest chain of martial arts centres and opened over 200 locations, thirty of these full-time. With such a big pool of students to choose from and because of my military and fighting background, I have been able to train multiple world champions and work with the very best in the industry.

Martial arts have always meant a great deal to me. When I struggled with dyslexia at school and didn't have much confidence in my abilities, martial arts were where I could excel and improve – it made me a better version of myself. Thanks to my martial arts training, I decided to become the man I wanted to be and do whatever was needed to achieve my goals. This led to my military career, and the trajectory of my whole life changed.

INTRODUCTION

Until now, we held our cards close to our chest and kept our success secrets in-house. That's how we have grown beyond our competitors and built the UK's largest chain of martial arts centres. Now I want to share my secrets with instructors outside my school, because sharing knowledge is a fundamental act of coaching. It's integral to martial arts as it allows us to pass on everything we know and to give something away without losing anything.

I want to show you what you need to become truly elite within your discipline and run the business you deserve. I have put together a system that has been used by thousands of other instructors before you to achieve their business goals alongside excellence in martial arts, regardless of the style they teach. All the systems, processes and mindsets are universal and will work anywhere in the Western world. Martial arts instructors love to teach, and the standard of martial arts teaching is higher now than it ever has been, but that alone isn't enough to run a successful school.

The main task of a martial arts instructor is to teach and to grow their students. But the first task is to recruit, sign up and retain students. As an instructor, you need to be a black belt in your discipline as well as a black belt in business. Your ability to run a business is as important to your success as the discipline you are teaching. A sustainable business is the only way your students can grow, otherwise, you won't have enough students to generate the income needed to look after yourself and your family, and you will accidentally and selflessly run yourself into the ground trying to help the students you do have. To truly serve your students, you need to master all the aspects of running a thriving school.

I have observed four main problems within the martial arts industry; you can remember these as the 4S's: sign-up, sustain, step back and stuck.

1. **Sign-up** – struggling to get enough students signing up each month. You need more signing up than are leaving.

2. **Sustain** – students who do join don't stay long enough. Based on my experience, the attrition rate of the average martial arts school is 6% monthly, and the majority of students that leave do so within the first twelve weeks of training.

3. **Step back** – the challenge of finding and training the right instructors for your team, as your business grows and expands, or just to allow you to step back from teaching to focus more on the business. The instructors who get burnt out are the ones who keep doing everything themselves.

4. **Stuck** – the cumulative effect of all of the above: lack of sign-ups means the schools don't make any money, so solo instructors can't afford to hire help and are stuck in a cycle of working day and night for little financial return.

INTRODUCTION

I wrote *Elite Martial Arts Instructor* so that instructors can compare their processes to those used in all my centres, see where the gaps are and then fill them. For instructors who are just starting out, it is a complete guide for launching and growing their schools. New instructors might find my methods easier to embrace as they don't have preconceived ideas of how to do things; instructors who are already teaching will have to re-steer a moving ship, which can be more challenging but always achievable. The reward will be a business that works for you and gives you the lifestyle you have always dreamed of. Regardless of how many Dans you have on your belt, regardless of how long you have been in business and regardless of how many students and centres you have right now, it's the white belt mentality that we have had installed into us from day one that makes us a success. We can always learn and we can always grow.

Elite Martial Arts Instructor will show you how to unlearn old habits and implement new ones into your daily, weekly and monthly routines. My system requires you to embrace the correct mindset, outline clear and concise goals and learn to fall in love with the processes so that there is quality in everything that you do. You will learn to think big and look for and attract the right people to work with to expand your team. You will be shown how to build your dream job and lifestyle and thrive in the chaos of growth. As you grow your school and/or open more locations, your students, black belts and instructors will perform better than ever before. While changes might well be met with resistance, *Elite Martial Arts Instructor* will show you how to get all existing students and families on board with your vision. As long as you trust the process, they will too.

My approach has a no-nonsense and no-compromises military flavour. I use examples from my time as a paratrooper, with a military analogy at the start of each 'round' in line with the goals. I have done this so that you will understand the mindset I have and how this has crossed over to success in fighting, coaching and business. I guarantee you will find it easy to understand – and even entertaining.

This book is based on the Six Rounds of Success, which are the processes of my training and selection course that I use for my franchise, British Military Martial Arts (BMMA). The goal of the Six Rounds is to make sure all of our instructors lead from the front and can do everything they ask their students to do and more. *Elite Martial Arts Instructor* will do for you what I do for my students: give you the physical and mental tools needed to succeed.

In the book, I have broken my Six Rounds of Success into three parts:

- Part One: Make It Grow
    - Round 1: Ready (Red On)
    - Round 2: Relaunch (Green On Go)

- Part Two: Make It Great
  - Round 3: Rapid Growth (Advance To Battle)
  - Round 4: Retention (The Battle)
- Part Three: Make A Difference
  - Round 5: Restructure (Reorg)
  - Round 6: Repeat (Training And Selection Of Staff)

If this sounds strenuous, it's because it is. Some of the ideas and approaches in *Elite Martial Arts Instructor* are extreme. But I am not offering you mediocrity. I am setting out a process for those who truly want to excel above others and be elite in all aspects of martial arts.

In my training course, which this book is based on, I picked the very best, who would go toe-to-toe with each other for five days in what was probably one of the hardest weeks of their lives. The military-style course would test their character as well as their martial arts skills, fitness and heart. They would be put through a shark tank sparring test, runs, log runs, fitness tests, written and practical teaching tests and more.

The book is a great way for people from any style of martial arts and of varying abilities to access information that was previously only available to elite instructors undergoing the selection process for my franchise. The book caters not only to you but to everyone, from the junior and senior instructors to the members of your administration team and others who want to support you on your journey to success.

How to use this book: read the whole book through, then return to Round 1 and begin implementing each stage, without compromise. You must complete every step exactly as described if you want the same results I have produced over and over again. Don't just do the easy parts, or the bits you like.

PART ONE
MAKE IT GROW

In this section, we go over the Ready and Relaunch rounds. In these rounds, we cover everything you need to know to start a school from scratch, right the way through to the launch event. We also learn how to relaunch your school and set it up for success if it's already open but not performing well.

The Evolution Of The Martial Arts Industry

Martial arts, for many people, has the potential to be more than just a hobby. It can be a lifestyle and a lucrative business that can benefit you, your family and your students. But many people don't know how to take their passion and skills in martial arts and turn it into a business. Similarly, there are many potential instructors who have the ability to teach, but don't see it in themselves or value themselves enough. As martial arts instructors, we inspire people by being the type of person they want to be. We're very important people in our student's lives. But we don't see that ourselves, so it's not surprising that the wider world doesn't realise it.

Since the 2008 recession hit in the UK, I've seen the martial arts industry moving backwards, and not much progress has been made. People are still charging similar prices for classes as they were twenty years ago, even though the quality of martial arts tuition has advanced remarkably in this time. There are more martial arts centres for sure, but the majority of the owners are not making enough money for the work they put in. Teaching martial arts and owning martial arts schools comes with a unique set of challenges, but these challenges can quite easily be met and overcome, as I will demonstrate, and we can enjoy success while doing what we love.

Before the recession in the 2000s, the martial arts industry was transforming. People were starting to teach for a living, and martial arts 'supercentres' began to open up. At that time, I had decided to leave the army and pursue a career in martial arts; it felt like an exciting moment to start my school. Successful school owners and gurus from the US came to give seminars on how to grow martial arts schools and businesses, and they were blowing UK school owners' minds with their level of entrepreneurship. While some of the ideas were a little over the top, many of the systems were profound, and the industry was full of success stories.

Not all the new processes I was learning were aligned with my personal values, but over the course of twenty-five years of teaching, I've eliminated what did not work for me and kept and improved upon the best methods for managing the dojo properly, and making it more professional and profitable. My personal experience as a fighter, a paratrooper, an army PTI, and a martial arts coach has fed into my system for growth and success in our industry, which is like no other in the world.

Parts of the process of running a martial arts business are common to any business. You have to know what the problems are and come up with solutions; you have to run your business more effectively and grow it through expansion, opening more schools so you make more money.

In the introduction, I identified the industry's four main problems, the things that stand in the way of school owners:

1. Sign-up – not being able to get enough students
2. Sustain – not keeping students long enough
3. Step back – not getting enough help to grow your team
4. Stuck – not making enough profit

I also introduced the Six Rounds of Success, which will give you the correct processes to address these problems, set up a school from scratch and expand your business. But alongside this, you need to develop the right mindset, discipline and follow-through in order to implement and sustain the changes.

Limiting beliefs and mindset

One of the biggest obstacles for martial artists who want to succeed in business is limiting beliefs and mindset. This is ironic when you consider the confidence and determination most martial artists develop during their training. But the focus that they have to develop to be at the top of their game in their chosen discipline doesn't always transfer to running a business. It is almost as if the two qualities, excellence in martial arts and excellence in entrepreneurship, are not meant to co-exist. There are several ways in which I see this happening.

First, a lot of martial artists feel that they are less devoted to their pupils and school if they make money. They almost feel guilty taking money for teaching. You won't have a successful business if you can't overcome this mindset. This internal conflict stems from a general sense of negativity in the industry around growth and money, even talking about it. This can be true of martial artists anywhere, but there is also a cultural element. Satisfaction with mediocrity is particularly evident in the UK and some parts of Europe compared with the US where success is welcomed and praised, and everyone thinks on a larger scale. In the UK, people who are thought to be 'too successful' or who 'show off' are not appreciated. Even if you don't want to be a failure, subconsciously you might not want to stand out by being 'too successful' or doing things 'too differently'.

Second, many outstanding martial artists are simply not interested in the business aspect of running a school, and are not interested in acquiring the skills. They aren't particularly interested in anything except martial arts. These instructors simply teach and run their businesses the way their instructors taught them. They don't network to learn about new business methods or trends and see what is working for the schools that are growing. Instructors will use the same syllabus they received from their instructor, even though there has been substantial improvement in knowledge of training methods, sports science, psychology and child development since they were first in a class.

This all adds up to a negative anti-success mindset, which can and will prevent you from growing your business. There is nothing wrong with making money, as long as you are doing it with integrity and not ripping off your students by selling them overly expensive packages they are not ready for, or enrolling them in classes that are inappropriate for their age or skill level.

Ideally, you want to make enough money as quickly as possible to sustain yourself and your family comfortably and to fund future growth for even bigger success. You don't want to have to borrow money (from the bank, your spouse, or your family and friends) to open or expand your school. In this book, I'll show you how you can do it all yourself so you are not over-leveraged.

Remember: any time you're taking money from people, you are in business. It can be a bad or a good business. If you aren't making money, no matter how good an instructor you are, it's a bad business. But if you are making a lot of money, it is a good business even if your martial arts skills suck. What I want to do with this book is align the two skills, so that we have great quality martial arts being taught in well-run, professional and profitable schools.

Instructors and school owners who aren't constantly working to improve their practice (networking, being mentored, informing themselves about new training methods, studying other schools) may well end up doing their students a disservice. This is because we don't know what we don't know.

The way many schools are run and the way the instructors are teaching has gone backward instead of moving forward. There is no accountability and school owners are lacking role models who are willing to share with them what they are doing and swap ideas. The reason I'm writing this book is to help transform the industry and bring it up a level for all of us, regardless of what martial arts style you teach.

It's important not to take any setbacks too personally. Many people commit to martial arts for intensely personal reasons. I certainly did. I moved schools and homes a lot, was always the new boy, and had to start over each time making new friends. I was six feet tall when I was thirteen and was often picked on by sixteen and seventeen-year-olds. I was still a boy but had to deal with situations involving young men.

On one occasion, when I was around fourteen, I got beaten up outside a shop for absolutely no reason, pushed to the floor and kicked in the face by a gang of seventeen and eighteen-year-olds. Even though I tried, I had no chance of fighting off so many of them, and they were so much older. I remember thinking while I was crying that I had to make myself so strong no one could ever hurt me again. This led me to commit to martial arts and then to join one of the toughest regiments in the military, as I never wanted to feel so vulnerable again.

The disappointment when your martial arts business does not thrive can feel disheartening. But if at first, you don't succeed, remember: if you have the passion and drive that you need, the rest is just business skills. You can learn these skills from this book. It's hard work, but follow my process and you will get there.

The 4S's

Let's return now to the four main problems encountered in this industry and discuss them in more detail.

1. Sign-up – not being able to get enough students. The main problem for most schools is the lack of new people coming through the doors. The secret is to have more students signing up every month than students who leave. To achieve this, you need a stream of inquiries coming in each day from multiple sources. This has become somewhat easier as social media has taken off. If you place a social media ad correctly and you're in a big enough town or city, you will get plenty of leads. But that's just the start; there are many steps between getting a lead and booking that person or family as an intro who shows up, signs up and stays.

There are so many other free ways of getting students into the school that have been lost over the years as school owners are picking the path of least resistance and putting up ads without doing much else. Without new students coming in, your school will close very quickly.

2. Sustain – not keeping students. Martial arts instructors today are competing with Xbox and PlayStation. Parents are busy and overworked and don't have the time to support their children like they used to. If you don't keep the whole family engaged, they will just drop off. The classes need to be dynamic and engaging to keep youngsters' attention and make them want to come back, right from that first class. And people need to feel they are in the right class for their age group and skill level.

3. Step back – not getting enough help to grow. If you are running the whole business solo, then you're only going to be able to grow to a certain size. You need enough instructors to help you expand the school or pull back from teaching to develop the business, network and attend seminars. If you have to wear all the hats while still on the hamster wheel of teaching, you will burn out. If you don't find the right help, you limit your potential for growth.

4. Stuck – not enough profit. Once again: if you are taking someone's money and providing them with a service, you are in business. If you are not taking in enough money, you are just not a very good business. You will end up running around all over the place without fair reward for the effort you put in. You will lose your passion for the martial arts as you get worn down and burnt out. Without enough profit, you won't be able to run your school effectively, which will do a massive disservice to your students.

Know your value

What I have noticed in over thirty-five years of martial arts training is that instructors don't value their skill set. This also happens in the military where people are highly skilled, but this is normalised as everyone else around them has the same skill set. Failing to see or doubting your value is also known as imposter syndrome. In martial arts, I meet very talented people all the time who are unaware of how much their skill set would be appreciated by others, so they undercharge for their services. This is also due to the mindset issue I identified earlier, where practitioners feel guilty about making a profit.

Think about what you have invested in your skill set as a martial arts teacher. You are likely to have trained a minimum of three to four times a week for ten years. That's around 3,120 to 4,160 hours of deliberate practice. You might have to drive thirty minutes each way to train, which doubles the time committed to your craft. On top, you go to tournaments, you pay for flights and hotels to compete abroad and you pay for gradings and seminars. You have invested thousands of pounds and hours into your discipline. Most people who aren't martial artists, top-level athletes or performers don't spend this amount of time and effort on anything. Just having made this investment and learning everything you have learned makes you exceptional.

If someone was to offer you £1million right now to surrender all the skills and knowledge you have, all the physical and mental benefits of your training, along with all the friends and experiences gained along the way, would you take the money? No. No amount of money could outweigh the benefits that you derive from your martial arts commitment.

So why is it that some instructors have an issue charging an amount that reflects their level of skill and value? Be as passionate about your business as you are about your discipline, recognise your worth and charge accordingly.

I want to see the industry coming together as a whole and not looking at each other as competitors, but as brothers and sisters working together to raise the industry up in the world. If everyone has good schools, we are all going to benefit. We need to network with each other and share ideas to make the entire industry as good as it can be. Together, we are a global force for good and positivity; our enemies are not one another, but the negative influences and distractions out there that are stopping people from reaching their full potential.

Multiple schools in one area

There are huge benefits to opening multiple schools in one area, and communicating this is one of the reasons I'm writing this book. I know from experience that having more martial arts schools in one area improves awareness and builds up all of the schools, and that is part of my method of expansion. I appoint 'area commanders' who open multiple schools (up to ten at a time) in one particular area. We have more success in towns where we have multiple schools than those where we just have one. We can share marketing between locations and get lots of referrals from students' friends and families across a wide area.

My first school in Telford (which today is our HQ and is run by chief instructor and area commander, James McCormick) had 400 students when I was teaching from there full-time with just me, one other instructor and the receptionist. Over the course of a few years, we built up to thirty other locations within a 10-mile radius. Because of this, everyone knew about us and we dominated the area. I'll tell you more about my area commander model later.

I'm sharing my methods now because I believe that a rising tide lifts all ships. There is enough potential for everyone to grow: we are currently only training 5% of primary school children. We don't need to compete with one another. It's not a zero-sum game.

James McCormick, who runs BMMA HQ, receiving his fourth Dan from Lee in 2022

I don't see other martial arts businesses as competitors. The real competitors today are social media, games and technology. What we need to do now is raise standards across the whole industry.

Summary

The four problems we face when running and growing a martial arts business include negativity around growth and money, not keeping students, not getting enough help to grow, and not making enough profit. My Six Rounds of Success, which will be presented in detail in this book, address each of these issues.

ROUND 1
Ready (Red On)

Round 1 includes the 'Ready' stage, which is all of the preparation that is needed to get everything ready before your first class, and for opening/relaunch night. Before you get started, first read the whole book so that you understand my Six Rounds method. Then return to this point and do everything I tell you, in the order that I tell you to do it. Don't move to the next round until you've completed this one.

The military analogy for this round is called 'Red on' because the red light at the aircraft exit, shown in the image on page 25, indicates to a paratrooper that the aircraft is approaching the place where it will dispatch the troops. A green light comes on when it's time to jump.

As a paratrooper, you will be waiting with all your kit on ready to jump for up to an hour, waiting for the red light. The kit (all the equipment, food and ammunition you need for the exercise or operation) will sometimes weigh as much as you. You will also be wearing your parachute, reserve parachute and helmet, with a weapon on you somewhere depending on the level of threat or exercise. You will be exhausted before you even get out of the aircraft.

If you are number one in the stick (the line of paratroopers ready to jump), you might be looking out of the open door into the unknown for five to ten minutes, which can feel like an eternity. If it's a night jump, you can't see a thing, just blackness and potential death. The noise of the plane is deafening and the smell of the diesel is sickening. You think of all the accidents that have happened and wonder if it will be you this time. You hear shouts and screams from all over the plane as the red light comes on. That's your fellow paratroopers psyching themselves up to jump after hours of nervous anticipation.

Then you remember who you are, an elite paratrooper, and all of the training you have done to get to this point. You surrender to the outcome and focus on your drills; you help the man to your front and back to distract yourself from your feelings. You know what's going to happen, but you can't do anything. Everything you should have done to prepare has to have been done by now. Thousands of checks will have taken place to ensure everything is exactly as it should be. You just need to get your mindset spot on.

This is the level of precision and attention to detail with which I approach my preparation for a relaunch, and it is how you must approach yours. When you reach Red On, there are no excuses or reasons why the things that need doing aren't done. If things aren't done or are done incorrectly, people can die.

In this round, I will outline exactly what needs to happen to prepare for the launch or relaunch of your school to 'Red on' standard. Everything needs to be done to the letter, with no adaptation, if you want to get the results that we get from our launches. We typically sign up forty to fifty new members on the first night, a hundred within two weeks, and two hundred within a month. This is the kind of success you can expect if you have done the appropriate preparation, which I will now outline.

Your business plan

Before you execute anything in the army, you get a detailed, comprehensive plan or set of orders. This might include a scale model of the attack scenario, and information about when and how the attack will happen. When you start your school, you need a plan with a similar level of detail.

You will need to know where you plan on starting your school, how many locations you will have and where they will be. You want to plan when your launch night will be, how much the launch will cost and, most importantly, how many students you need to sign up to break even and then start making profit.

The best way to do this is to write a comprehensive business plan to help you understand what needs to happen and when. You can get free business plan templates online. A good business plan should contain a summary of your company and market analysis – for example, are there already martial arts schools in your area doing well? If so, that's a great sign. As I have said, there's room for everyone. It should also set out your proposed organisational and management structure (who is doing what?), what services you'll offer, your prices and a financial plan.

Your mission statement

Along with your business plan, now is the time to think about what your mission statement is. This is a statement that you will live by and that you can show your staff and instructors so they can all buy into it. If your statement is to earn as much money as you can so you can buy a Lamborghini, the staff might not buy into this. Think about your 'why', about what motivates you to get up in the mornings and how you want to make an impact on others.

If you are just about to start out, your mission statement now will be different from what you would write in a couple of years' time, when you have a full-time centre and multiple locations. For example, my current mission statement is: 'To inspire and educate as many people as possible to teach martial arts professionally, so they can positively impact as many lives as possible around the world.'

Notice I have made my statement about what I want to do for others, not myself. The main things that should be reflected in a mission statement are values, ethics, inspiration, goals and company culture. It shouldn't be more than a couple of sentences. It will take you a bit longer than you think, and you will keep changing it and fine-tuning it. It's important to keep your mission statement where you will see it regularly (on the wall, or a screensaver) so that you communicate your brand clearly and stay aligned with your core values as you grow.

Your financial plan

My financial planner has been one of the most transformational tools I have ever used. It has literally changed my life – previously, I was turning over lots of money but always seemed to run out at the end of the month. I now understand my cash flow and budget and I'm able to save and have a reserve of cash in the bank. I pay myself properly (and first) and still have enough left over for everything else. If you're not creating and using a financial plan, then you are still just playing at your business and will not reach your full potential.

If you have ever dieted before and tried to estimate what you're eating and play about with your training, doing what you feel like, you'll know that you never get the same results as when you get an app on your phone and log everything that you eat according to your nutritional plan, and then follow the complementary training programme that was assigned with the diet. It's exactly the same with financial planning for your business: the details matter and you need to have accountability.

Learning to do profit and loss (P&L) projections will make you accountable to the business and is a good discipline to acquire even if you don't think you need to yet. You can make a basic monthly P&L statement on a spreadsheet easily; it needs to show what money is coming in, what's going out and what's left at the end of each month. A yearly budget is a little more complicated: you do the same P&L for each month, but you'll need to 'project' the future months, estimating how many students you think you will have and at which stage.

I had to learn to deal with P&Ls overnight when we acquired an equipment company called Kicksport, as we'd partnered with venture capitalists and had to show them what was happening to their money. It was such a useful exercise that I still do a P&L projection every year to see where I can expect to be. I also do it monthly for each of the locations I own and my franchise business, to show me in black and white how much each school is making and whether we are on track to reach our goals. If some schools aren't making enough, I know where I need to put my attention.

On my website www.leematthewsofficial.com you can book a free session with one of our team who will help you put together a 12-month P&L that is specific to your requirements, with all of the information about your school along with your plans and goals.

The white belt mindset

A beginner, or white belt, is extremely open to learning, willing to learn from everybody. This is because, as a beginner, you don't have an ego. You can only learn when you are humble. If you think you are right all the time and know everything, then you shut yourself off from learning. It is important when reading this book (or even as a black belt, instructor or champion) to keep a white belt mindset.

According to the unconscious/conscious competence model, there are four stages to the learning process, which reflect our level of understanding of the information that is being given to us. We can relate this to our comprehension of techniques and skill levels in martial arts.

Stage 1 – Unconscious Incompetence. We don't know what we don't know. This is a complete lack of knowledge in a subject or field, which ironically often leads to people assuming they know more about a subject than they do. You may have heard the name of a martial art, but don't know the first thing about it. You could even be completely unaware of its existence.

Stage 2 – Conscious Incompetence. When you become aware of how much you have to learn, this is where true learning begins. You realise that things aren't always as easy as they look. This is a beginner stage, where you come to understand that skill and success only come with consistent practice. For example, you turn up to your first martial arts class and roll or spar with a senior grade and realise how vulnerable you are. This sense of incompetence can be very uncomfortable for some people, while others might be excited at the prospect of so much to learn. If you're used to a high level of competence in your discipline, it can be a shock to recognise how little you know about business.

Stage 3 – Conscious Competence. This is where we work at what we don't know. We know what is required to get better at something and we work towards gaining a level of mastery. In a martial arts context, this might mean you are able to do the moves or remember the sequence, but you have to think and concentrate before you are able to execute them to a reasonable level.

Stage 4 – Unconscious Competence. At this final stage, you no longer need to think about what move to throw or how you are going to do it. Perfect action comes without thought. You see this with top-level athletes and performers and speakers. In business, this could mean knowing all the right steps to take toward making a decision because you have made many similar decisions in the past.

UNCONSCIOUS INCOMPETENCE	UNCONSCIOUS COMPETENCE
You're not very good at something but have no idea as you've never tried it before.	Mastery of the technique is achieved, and you can perform it well without effort or thought.
CONSCIOUS INCOMPETENCE	**CONSCIOUS COMPETENCE**
You try something for the first time and realise how bad at it you are.	With thought and effort, correct technique can be achieved.

Any true master of their art is unconsciously competent. There are varying opinions on exactly how long it takes to reach this stage, but according to Matthew Syed, unconscious competence will take thousands and thousands of hours of repetition, and to achieve mastery requires around 10,000 hours of careful, concentrated practice with the intent to improve.[1] Syed argues that mastery can be achieved by anyone, regardless of genetics, if they practise long enough in the correct environment with the right coaches.

As we follow the steps through from preparation to launch, I will introduce a few key concepts and core business skills that will help you improve your competence. First up, is prioritisation.

How to prioritise

Martial arts instructors are not good with their time. They typically spend long evenings in the dojo and get to bed quite late. The time they allocate to working on their business tends to be on weekdays, but after fitting in their own training this leaves a shorter working day – you will normally need to start getting ready for classes in the early afternoon.

To make the most of a short working day you need to be organised and prioritise well. I have observed a

---

[1] M Syed, *Bounce: The myth of talent and the power of practice* (Fourth Estate, 2010)

tendency among new businesses to follow the noise when choosing the order of tasks to do. That might seem the most productive way to do things, but it's not necessarily the most efficient.

A useful and widely used tool for increasing your productivity in a way that will drive your business forward is Stephen Covey's Time Management Matrix.[2] The matrix is made up of four quadrants, and everything that you might choose to spend your time on falls into one of these quadrants:

- **Not urgent, not important:** Scrolling through social media, reading irrelevant emails, having trivial conversations with work colleagues, instructors and friends etc. These activities are basically just passing time, with no clear direction or purpose – maybe it's not even fun. You should be aware of how much time you are spending in this quadrant.

- **Urgent, not important:** On some days you might feel that you spend most of your time in this quadrant. It's where you deal with everyday interruptions that you feel the need to respond to in the moment, such as answering calls and returning messages, though these tasks bear little or no relevance to your future goals. These might be requests from friends and family and some

---

[2] S Covey, *The 7 Habits of Highly Effective People: Powerful lessons in personal change* (Free Press, 2004)

might be from students or your team. It can feel like these things need your attention right now, but be aware that stopping to deal with them is taking your focus away from your ultimate goal.

- **Urgent and important:** An example of things that fall into this category is emergencies that you must deal with personally, which can ruin your plans for productive work with a longer-term focus. I call these fastballs: important phone calls, addressing a complaint, finding last-minute cover for classes. These things can't be put off and they do need to be actioned, but can you put systems in place to make these easier to deal with or delegate?

- **Not urgent but important:** This is the most productive quadrant to be in. Examples of activities in this area are developing your syllabus, training your team and making your business plan and financial plan. You will also need time for your strategy: goal setting, visualising and planning your next big move. All this requires calm, focused attention – it is not helpful to be stressed or rushed. Your plan for each day should include tasks that fall into this quadrant and try to ensure that you prioritise them. If you can be productive in this area each day, you will see a difference. When I get up, I put my phone in airplane mode, avoid my email inbox and go straight to the 'not urgent but important' task of the day: that's what I'm doing now, writing this book. It's easy to neglect these tasks when you are dealing with urgent and important tasks, but a lot of the tasks in this quadrant will become 'urgent and important' if neglected. Worse, some will never get done, which is wasted potential.

In an ideal world, you would have few emergencies because most tasks would be addressed while they are 'not urgent but important'. Life has its own plans sometimes but when you prioritise, you are helping to prevent emergencies before they happen and develop and grow outside of your comfort zone.

	URGENT	NON-URGENT
IMPORTANT	Crisis Pressing problems Deadline driven projects	Relationship building Finding new opportunities Long-term planning Preventitive activities Personal growth Recreation
NOT IMPORTANT	Interruptions Emails, calls, meetings Popular actitivies Pressing matters	Trivia, busy work Time wasters Some calls & emails Pleasant activities

Preparing to launch a school

Another useful tool that will help you in business is the Pareto principle, otherwise known as the 80/20 rule.[3] The basic idea of this rule is that input doesn't equal output. For example, 80% of the time you wear the same 20% of your clothes; 80% of your problems come from 20% of your people; 80% of your customers come from 20% of your marketing; and when competing, you use 20% of the available techniques 80% of the time.

When applied to your business, the Pareto principle means that there is a small proportion of your input (or effort) that creates most of the output (or results). For example, if you spend £1,000 on marketing each month, equally spread across ten different tools and platforms (flyers, posters, Facebook ads, local paper ads and so on), then you won't find that each £100 spent generates the same return. Rather, you would most likely get 80% of the results from 20% of the marketing spend (£200). Once you can identify what this 20% is, you can change how you spend your other £800, either saving it or redirecting it all to the 20% that gets the best results.

In my business, 80% of our students are primary school age, so when we launch a new school, we base ourselves in or near a primary school. This gives us

---

3   V Pareto *Cours D'économie Politique* (Rouge, 1896)

the most potential new students within easy travelling distance. In this case, I'm putting 100% of my effort where it will deliver the most reward.

What are you spending the most money and time on in your business, and what is the outcome? If there is one part of your business generating the most problems or difficult customers and it's taking up too much of your time, can you eliminate that troublesome area? When the Pareto principle is properly understood and applied it can change your life and your business. It is especially applicable to launching a new school. There is a lot to do before a launch, but follow my method step by step and you will get results.

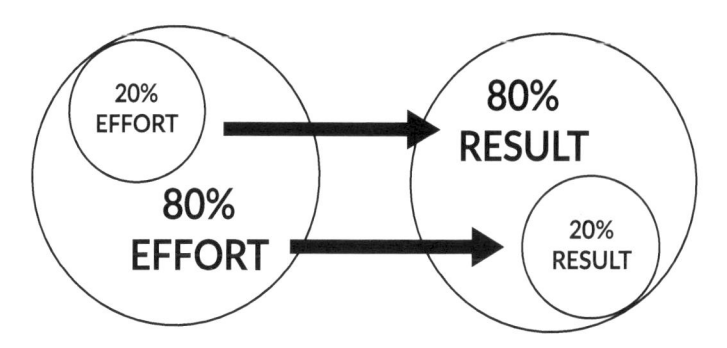

Location selection

Ideally, if you're starting a martial arts school from scratch or only have a few students, you will launch in primary schools. You should look for schools with 300 pupils or more. You can expect to sign up 5% to 10% of the children in the school, so a launch in a smaller school won't be as effective. When I launch in an area, we get the instructors to find up to ten primary school locations of this calibre and run launch classes in each. They will typically do two locations a night: an early class at around 3.30pm for kids aged four to seven, then a class for the eight to eleven-year-olds straight after. There is then enough time to drive to another primary school with 300 or more students and start classes at 6pm with the age four-to-seven group first, the eight-to-eleven group next and then adults or ladies-only to finish. Instructors who do this five days a week can expect to get around 200 sign-ups (twenty per location) over the course of all ten launches. For a launch of this scale, I would expect it to take about four weeks from the 'Green on "go"' stage.

When selecting your launch locations, only work with schools that will allow you to run an assembly. The assembly needs to be no more than a week before your launch. At the assembly, you'll invite the children to an evening or after-school class – this is the launch night, which parents must also attend. You also need the school to agree in advance to help you promote the launch by distributing flyers and sending texts, emails and parent mail app messages to parents (which can be as simple as 'martial arts classes starting soon' followed by your mobile number and the launch date and time). Before the assembly, deliver flyers to the school in bundles of thirty, making it as easy as you can for the schools to distribute them. We ask the school to send parents a reminder text on the assembly day. You need to agree all of this at the start – schools are busy and you might have to be quite firm and persistent to get them to cooperate with everything you need. I find it's best to just be honest and say, 'For us to launch successfully, we need to do all of these things,' then if they say no, you can ask another school and only work with the most helpful ones.

We get permission to be at the school gates at 3.15pm on the day of the assembly to speak to parents and book the students in there and then. We turn up in uniform (no coats, even if it's cold – we want to stand out and be seen) with our clipboards to sign people up. After the assembly, your phone will blow up with calls and text messages. You still have to work to turn those enquiries into students, so make sure you respond to every single enquiry as if it's the most important thing in the world. Answer questions but try and direct them into coming for a free intro session the following week where you will be able to answer all questions in person.

Once you have successfully launched in schools you will have money coming in and, after a few months, a group of committed students. At this point, we would look at the busiest areas if we wanted to move into a full-time location. I wouldn't recommend moving straight into one without first having the students, as you can use the cash flow from these to support your next move.

Branding/marketing

Make sure your branding is consistent across all media platforms. If you're already part of a franchise that's working with a marketing agency or has in-house expertise, that's great. If not, you've got to make everything clear. Make sure that your messaging talks about the values you promote and the benefits of martial arts for your potential students. It shouldn't be about how hard you are or how many bricks you can break over your head. Some children might be impressed by that, but your messaging is targeted at their parents.

Online

Your website must be kept updated with all relevant information. This includes location, days and times of training, contact information and a simple booking form. Make sure your website is consistent with the rest of your online presence; include links to other platforms such as Facebook and Instagram accounts. Put your website link on the flyers that you give out on launch day. Also, prepare professional-looking ads for social media; this advertising needs to be live around four weeks ahead of your launch.

Promotional assemblies

As well as your launch assembly, you should run regular promotional assemblies. The content of the assemblies will depend on your style of martial arts and what you do, but the goal is to be entertaining for the children while communicating a message that has value. At our assemblies, we talk a lot about self-control and respect. We normally play a guessing game where we demonstrate a few different moves, such as snap punch, reverse punch and spin kick. We then ask the children to guess if one of these is the most important move in martial arts. Then we bow and tell them, 'The bow is the most important move in martial arts because it shows respect.' We bring mats and pads and invite children to go through some drills. We show them the relaxed position and attention position, bowing throughout the demo and creating a sense of urgency and high energy. For older children, we do a boys versus girls competition and see which team can throw the most punches in ten seconds, using this as a way to talk about what competition is and why it's important.

Booking and confirmation

The booking process is extremely important. After a promotional assembly, you will be inundated with messages and calls. But you've got to keep the energy high until the launch and remember that you still have to work to turn enquiries into students.

When booking, be sure to get a parent's phone number and email address. Then send a confirmation letting them know that you will be contacting them twenty-four hours before the launch to reconfirm. We use billing companies for the booking process; this allows us to book people straight into an online platform, which then turns into an electronic online debit. But you can use pen and paper if you prefer – choose whatever system, digital or manual, suits you.

If you've done your assembly well, you will get a lot of parents booking for your launch, but if you don't confirm them properly most of the kids won't turn up. Whichever way they've contacted you – email, phone call, text message – use the same form of communication to get back to them and collect their details. Getting confirmation in the twenty-four hours before launch is the most important part of the sales process. This is how you set the parents up for a successful sale.

Let them know that you are oversubscribed and that there will be a special offer available at the launch class for the first twenty people who turn up, and that more than that are booked in. If you do everything right, you will have more than twenty just at that class – if not, you will still have more than twenty that you can reference across all of the evening classes. You want to make sure you have

READY (RED ON)

leverage. Tell them in the confirmation text what the special offer is going to be and what your joining fee offer is, so that there are no surprises. Don't talk about the price of the lessons until the launch night. Once people have seen your classes in practice, they will form an emotional connection and be ready to buy. If they ask about the price before the launch, just say you will go over all the details on the night as it depends on which programme or how many classes they book. If they push for more, break the monthly fee into a price per class, but try to avoid going into detail just yet.

Create urgency through the twenty-four hours before launch. The text message that is sent out the night before should give the full address (including postcode), date and time of the class and a request: 'Please confirm your attendance, as we are fully booked. Text back "yes" to confirm your spot.' You must require that they respond in order to keep their spot. In the morning, you won't have a response from everyone, so re-send the text message to those who haven't replied. At midday, call any who still haven't responded. By doing this, you know exactly who will be there on launch night. You will also need to make sure you tell them to bring a method of payment and their bank details if they want to take advantage of the special offer, then explain what that is. Then sign off with your name.

Embrace the chaos

According to Murphy's Three Laws:

1. Anything that can go wrong will go wrong.
2. Nothing is as easy as it looks.
3. Everything takes longer than you think it will.[4]

Whatever can go wrong in your launch, will – at least once. When it does, don't be fazed by it; understand that this is part of the process, work around it and make notes of what you can tweak next time.

You will probably find the first launch stressful, and there is more stress to come as you grow your business. Being successful sometimes feels like fear, pain, apprehension and exhaustion. You will still be aligned with your purpose so will feel on track in life, but to be successful you have to push yourself and it will be a struggle. On reflection, I've been happiest when I've been challenged and engaged in a struggle but knowing I'm headed in the right direction, in line with my values and life mission.

Learn to live in the chaos. Welcome stress into your life and learn to build up your tolerance to stress over time, so that what was once a big problem will seem

---

4 EA Murphy, 'An engineer's report – what every "operator" should know', Aerospace Medical Research Laboratory, Wright-Patterson Air Force Base, OH (1969)

manageable. Most people are used to a default level of happiness and quickly become unhappy and stressed when a problem appears. Their happiness or mental stability is determined by how many problems they have. A series of problems (which is basically life in business) will cause them extreme stress and eventually lead them to break down. You can only grow as big as your ability to manage stress; if you try to avoid stress, you will limit yourself.

You need to seek out problems – or challenges, as I like to call them. Find problems before they find you and dive right into the heart of them. Look honestly at what is there, even if you don't like what you see. You will then be in a position to move to a better place. If you don't know where you are, you won't know which way to go. Learn to live in the free fall and you will soon realise that 99% of problems get solved. In a lot of cases, something that was going pear-shaped, with a bit of outside-the-box resourceful thinking, can be turned into something better than the original plan.

Soon, you won't have to wait for problems to be solved to reach your default level of happiness or contentment. You can be happy in the eye of the storm. After a few years of this type of mental conditioning (not dissimilar to physical training), problems lose their power over you. It's like life has had the stress volume turned right down; this is the secret to having more peace in your life.

I used to think of problems in a negative way. I would be anticipating problems in every incoming phone call, email or text, subconsciously willing them into my life. I would be constantly ticking over on a stress level of 70–80%, just waiting for something to go wrong to send me over the edge. I now idle at around 30% and the problems just don't seem to be there like they used to. I am dealing with multiple issues daily and some can take weeks or months to resolve, but they hold no power over me – I look at them as opportunities to improve.

As soon as I get news of a potential problem, I immediately ask myself what the worst-case scenario could be, financially and emotionally, and accept it. I consider what I could do to take the sting out of it, and then do everything I can do to stop the worst-case scenario from happening. Almost every time I do this, I manage to resolve the situation or find a compromise of some sort. That then feels like a win, as I had already accepted the worst outcome. Change your mind and your thinking and you change or get rid of the issue. The problem is the mindset, not the 'problem'.

The more problems (challenges) you have in your life and that you ultimately resolve, the better your life will be. You become successful by solving one thing at a time, with the benefits compounded over time.

In business, you can and will experience every type of problem there is, from betrayal by friends, loss of money, lack of cash and things falling through that you thought were done deals. These are all part of everyday life in business. They are not problems in the way that things going wrong at home or with your family are. You are not truly successful in business until everything that can go wrong has gone wrong, on multiple occasions, and you're still standing, stronger than ever. Remember, Neo first had to die in *The Matrix* before he could be born again as The One.

While it's important to be aware of potential problems, you need to avoid 'analysis paralysis', as identified by Igor Ansoff.[5] This is when you spend so much time thinking of everything that could go wrong that you stand still, afraid to make a move. But life is going to happen, whether you take that next step or not.

Finally, after we've done all this preparation it is important to act and follow through. A lot of people start the preparation and don't finish it, but every single person that completes the 'Red on' stage and makes it to 'Green on "go"' on launch night will have 100% success.

Summary

In this round, we've been preparing to jump. We've gone through all of the preparation necessary leading up to the launch (or relaunch) of your school. We've

---

5   IH Ansoff, *Corporate Strategy: An analytic approach to business policy for growth and expansion* (McGraw-Hill, 1965)

covered everything you need to know to run a successful assembly in a primary school and get the word out about your new school. We've talked about how to book students in a thorough way that ensures maximum attendance by people who are primed to join. The next round covers 'Green on "go"', which is the actual launch or relaunch of your new school.

ROUND 2
Relaunch (Green On 'Go')

In this round, we will be discussing everything you need to do on your launch or relaunch night, in detail. The launch night is your first actual night teaching using all of your new systems. The military analogy for this is 'Green on "go"'.

You're standing in the plane full of anticipation when the red light appears. Everyone is in position. Everything has been checked at least three times. You have done everything possible to be ready for the problems that will inevitably occur. You are no longer worried, as you know everything that can be done, has been done. It is at this point that you let go mentally and totally surrender. If you think of what could go wrong, you will not jump. You will do what the body wants in this situation and run away or freeze.

In this situation, I would sometimes be so scared that I worried I would freeze and not remember my drills. But as soon as the red light comes on, you forget the worry and become an invincible and un-killable paratrooper. After what seems like an eternity, you're suddenly thrust into instant action.

The moment when all the stars align is when the green light appears. Everything is where it should be in this perfect moment of chaos. Number one is at the door and the PJIs (parachute jump instructors) are watching the light as if their life depends on it. When it turns green, you hear their words echoing through the plane. 'Go!' Both plane doors are open, so the wind and engine noise are deafening. There are shouts of aggression and commitment from the other men in the plane as you move closer and closer to the aircraft door with purpose and intention. You're holding your kit with both hands in front of your body. This is difficult, as it is awkwardly placed resting on your legs. You get closer to the door and see a PJI guiding the paratroopers one at a time towards the door. They push them on the back to dispatch them out of the plane with enough momentum to dive out and avoid sliding down the side of the plane and twisting up the rigging lines.

The PJI must be precise. Paratroopers are dispatched out of the port side with a one-second delay, so you must be no more than one second away from the man in front of you. The same is happening on the starboard side. There should be a half-second delay between the two sides of the plane. If both sides dispatch at the same time, the paratroopers will meet at the back of the plane as their parachutes deploy. The chutes can wrap around each other, and both men will plummet toward the ground without a properly deployed parachute. Even if they try to pull their reserve parachute, it will wrap around the mess of chutes as they hurtle towards the ground.

As you approach the door for your turn, you hear the PJIs shout, 'Go! Go!' You see the guy in front of you move towards the door, then turn and hand his static line to the PJI before jumping and getting sucked out of the exit that barely looks big enough to fit through. It's your turn now to hand them your static line, turn and jump. You experience the biggest adrenaline rush you can imagine. You jump away from the loud controlled chaos as you shout out your drills, '1,000, 2,000, 3,000,' and check your canopy as the engine of the plane gets quieter the farther away you get. You check above your head and the canopy seems to be in good order. That's the first win. You enjoy a moment of stillness before continuing with your drills.

You hear distant shouts from other paratroopers in the sky as they shout to each other to steer away. If two paratroopers' parachutes deploy, and they are occupying the same air space, you can get what's called an air steal. This is when the canopy of one parachute steals the air of the parachute above it. This can collapse the parachute and the soldier will fall until he is far enough below to get his own air space. Then it will re-open – and steal the air back from the other parachute. This will keep happening until one of them falls to the floor. Every paratrooper has stories of when they or someone around them experienced an air steal or a near miss in the sky or on the ground.

To avoid this, as soon as the parachute opens, you look around and perform your next drill, making sure no one is near you. If someone is close, you shout to steer away while grabbing half of the rigging lines to collapse one side of your parachute to encourage it to move away. Once you're in a clear space, you need to release your kit, so you check below. Once you unclip it, it falls beneath you and hangs a few metres below on a rope. You must release both hooks at the same time, or it jams. If you only release one side, all the weight will be on one hook, making it nearly impossible to release because of the weight and having limited leverage and strength while in the air. You don't want to land with your kit still attached because it's in front of your legs. If you land forward, you won't be able to bend your legs and could break them.

A successful release is another win. Now on to the next drill. You look in the direction you are heading to detect any obstacles, and try to steer away. You don't have much time when you're jumping from 1,000 feet – even lower on operational jumps. From exit to landing, you are in the air for no longer than forty-five to sixty seconds. You've revised and practised your drills over and over again to the point of utter boredom. You need to be able to do them unconsciously when you are scared and there is potential danger everywhere.

You come in for the landing. You get into the appropriate position and look to the horizon, waiting to hit the floor. You don't look down, as you will get a ground rush and could end up reaching for the floor in anticipation. Moving your ankles and feet out of their correct position could cause injury. You hear your kit hit the floor and know that a second later it will be you. You tuck into a tight position and accept the landing. You hit the floor and continue to roll with momentum. Not dissimilar in purpose to a judo or jiu-jitsu break fall/roll, but with arms tucked in tight over the reserve parachute that is clipped into your chest, chin tucked down.

You do another half roll and land on your back, looking up at the sky. You made it. After a brief moment of relief, you collapse the parachute as quickly as possible, detach it and get it rolled up. Otherwise, you could get dragged all over the DZ (Drop Zone). Now you've hit the floor, you can start your real job of getting to the objective or attack.

The 'Green on "go"' stage of the Six Rounds of Success is the relaunch or launch night. This is when all the preparation has been done and it's time to jump into action. We will run our launch night with the same precision as we do in the execution of a military mission.

Beware negativity

Make sure that you surround yourself with positive and motivated people. It's even better if the people you spend most of your time with are more successful than you in the area you want to succeed in. You are the mean average of the five people you spend the most time with. There isn't much time in the day if you're grinding to be successful. This might sound harsh, but anyone you spend time with must add value to your life. When you're young, you're happy to hang out with anyone just for the company and safety in numbers, but as you get older and have less free time available, as well as clear goals you want to achieve, your time is more precious. That means everyone must add value in some way. That could be in making you laugh, which is important. Maybe they are loyal and always have your back. Perhaps they are the group organiser and make shit happen. They could be ahead of the game in life and being around them motivates you.

You need to make sure that you, in turn, add value to your friends, so that more people of a higher calibre will want to be around you. Your friends should be happy and excited about your success and support your big ideas, not tear you down. Sometimes the most negative people can be your family. You need to be honest with them and make them see how their comments, habits and patterns are detrimental to your goals. It is important, though, to listen to people whose opinions you respect. Specifically, it is the people who are experts in their area that you should be listening to, not everyone else – as everyone has an opinion about everything these days.

Some people are not conscious of how negative they can be. If one of your friends is unconsciously negative, you can point this out to them. But if they don't listen, minimise the time you spend around them so that you won't pick up this mindset. Some people are hardwired to only see the negative. It's up to you to decide how you look at something. If you want to be productive, the best way to look at something is the way that empowers you to take action. This doesn't mean not looking at things as they really are and burying your head in the sand. It's important that you recognise the reality of a situation and understand the consequences, but focus on the outcome you want to achieve and how you can get there.

Negativity spreads quicker than positivity. You always hear about the demise or destruction of someone's career quicker than you do if they win something or a great thing happens. People seem to love bad news. In the UK, you can almost guarantee that if a stranger speaks to you, it will be to moan about the weather, or the train being late. One negative person in your school or club can bring the whole house down. They can turn people against each other and get parents riled up about something that only they were annoyed about. You will definitely experience this, so it's important that if you have this type of person in your club (or indeed your life), you remove them immediately. It doesn't matter how many chances you give them. They will quiet down for a bit but eventually start up again with the negativity.

I've seen schools destroyed by this and big groups of students break off and leave. If this happens, it is because of weak leadership. It is always one person doing most of the damage. Find out who they are and get them away from everyone else. Let them know that you don't believe they share the same values as your school and politely wish them the best in their future endeavours. Everyone else will soon find out what you've done and, if they were following a similar path, they will quickly adjust their behaviour to avoid the same fate. This is great for retention and shows your strength as a leader. Once the negative person has left, make sure you don't talk badly about them, or you will be playing into that same negativity. Only ever speak highly of people, or not at all. Never complain to anyone in your school about anything negative that occurs, just take action.

When I was at the end of my basic training as a paratrooper, we went to the RAF camp Brize Norton where we learned to become military parachutists. It's four weeks with great food, women allowed on base and a nightclub. It is nothing like the normal life of a trainee paratrooper. You start with an easy jump in a small sky van where very little can go wrong, to help you get used to falling and doing drills correctly. Next are single-stick jumps from one side of the bigger C130 aircraft, then simultaneous sticks from both sides of the craft ('sim sticks'). Eventually, you perform equipment jumps, a single stick, a sim stick and, finally, a night jump.

One of the guys from our platoon was an older recruit and highly competent. He had completed the first couple of jumps, and we were on our first equipment jump. This is where things can start to go wrong if you're not confident with your drills. He was number one in the door so everyone else would jump after him. I was a few men behind him when the red light came on. We got ready, the green light appeared – but nothing happened. There was some commotion for a few moments while we all figured it out – he was totally terrified and refusing to jump.

The green light went off and the plane circled around. They unclipped and separated him. Then they checked us, did another approach and dispatched us over the Weston-on-the-Green DZ.

As a paratrooper, we get read the green light warning order every time we jump. This is to ensure we understand the consequences of not jumping. If you refuse in an operational context, you stop the whole mission and will go to prison. Since this was training, he didn't go to prison. But we never saw him again.

We all jumped, re-kitted and jumped again. By the time we got back, his locker had been cleared out. He was one of the best recruits in the platoon, but the army knows the effect that negativity has on a group, so this is the standard process for anyone who refuses to jump. I was more scared of the consequences I'd face for not jumping than I was of the jump itself. You have to believe in the process and your drills, regardless of anything else, and have full confidence in the process.

You will find that success attracts success, and negativity attracts negativity. I've had groups of students leave and go to another school in my area just before taking the black belt test, because the kids or parents thought our test was too hard. I'm not sure they consciously knew this, but that was the reason. I am sure they enjoyed the new school and it was more suited to their mindset. I used to feel insecure about students leaving, but I then realised that the elite gravitate to each other just as the weak do.

Balance versus counterbalance

A world champion is not a balanced person. A paratrooper is not a balanced person. A top businessman or woman is not a balanced person. You don't open 200 kickboxing locations by being balanced. Are you starting to get it?

You have to be the opposite of balanced to excel at anything. If you're not, someone else will be and they will get ahead of you. You need to be selfish and totally immerse yourself in what you're doing. You need to live, breathe and dream about it. Every thought you have should be about it. Talk about it with others who are as passionate about it as you are. If they aren't, change your circles.

As a fighter, I used to try and do what I thought everyone else would not be doing. This meant training sessions on Friday and Saturday evenings and on

Christmas morning. Anything and everything to get the edge.

In my life, I've had the privilege to compete at the highest level in my sport, which is kickboxing/sport karate. Every single person who manages to get on their national team had to work their way to the top. They have to be the champion of their country, and there could be three or four people in each weight class all capable of winning. If they win and go to the World Championships, every single person that they fight will be a champion of their own country – there will be many possible winners.

If you're not doing everything you possibly can to get even the smallest advantage, you won't win. There can be no balance. There can be no skipping a class or tournament. Everything has consequences. It's not the fact of missing a training session that's the problem, it's the mindset that allowed you to find an excuse to miss it. Excuses will become a habit if you aren't careful, and this will be your downfall.

Standing in front of an opponent at a world or European championships, I always knew that I was the fittest and had trained harder. That was the one thing I could always rely on. Not being able to believe that I had trained harder would have put me at a disadvantage, so I made sure I always did.

RELAUNCH (GREEN ON 'GO')

You are never going to be a champion or a paratrooper if you have a 'balanced' life and eat healthily only on some days, and only train for half the week. You can always be and do more, so do and be it. Don't let someone else get the glory.

If I can't lead a balanced life, does that mean I can never rest, never eat tasty food and never take my girlfriend or boyfriend out? No, of course not. What I have learned as I've got older, got married and had kids is how to counterbalance. This isn't something you often hear normal people say, but let's be honest, if you're reading this book it's because you don't want to be normal. You want to be exceptional.

Most people compromise, which means everyone loses. You want a win-win. This is what counterbalancing provides. What I do is throw myself into a task completely and fully submerge myself in it. Then I counterbalance this by submerging myself back into my family, resting or a break. For example, when I was training for a tournament or away on tour with the army, I would automatically submerge back into family life when I returned. If you have been training like a demon for a big tournament, training twice a day sometimes and dropping weight, then after the fight, make sure you rest and eat well. Plan something to look forward to when you've done what you need to do. Then, turn your phone off and be 100% present for it. This doesn't mean going from one extreme to the other, but make sure you counterbalance so that you get the most from all aspects of your life.

As we used to say in the Parachute Regiment, 'Work hard, play harder.' We would work and play equally hard, but we always worked more than we played. For those who didn't, it became pretty unpleasant.

Executing on a plan

'Have a plan and stick to it,' is a common piece of advice. I agree with it, to a certain extent. But there is another way of looking at things, one that is a lot more realistic and can motivate you when things go wrong, which they always do. In the military, there is an alternative saying: 'No plan survives contact.' Mike Tyson seemingly shared this view, saying: 'Everyone has a plan until they get punched in the face.'[6]

While this is true, it doesn't mean you shouldn't have a plan. It means you need to have a solid plan that will hold up under pressure. Your plan needs to be able to change as you move forward – you can't predict the future and will need to adapt and respond as things start to unfold in the real world. The objective of your plan always stays the same. To win the battle or fight, you must have an action plan. But continually test and adjust as you go along.

---

6   M Tyson, *The Way of the Fight* (Blue Rider Press, 2013)

Murphy's first law summarises this well: 'Anything that can go wrong, will.' Whenever you set a goal or have an important task to achieve, things will go wrong. This is normal and part of the process. I've seen this happen a lot when fighting and coaching. If you'd made it to a big championship final, you could guarantee that something would be wrong. There would be a referee that the fighter didn't like, an injury, or a lack of sleep the night before.

I saw it in the military too, especially in P Company during the selection stages. Not sleeping because of nerves and/or injuries was common. For some, these were the reasons they failed; for others, they were just another challenge that had to be overcome. Once you achieve something big, you soon start to realise that this is part of the process and part of success. With your school launch, if and when things go wrong, dig in and push on knowing that even if the plan doesn't survive contact, your objective will be achieved.

H-hour: The launch event

In the military, H-hour is the hour for launching an operation. In this case, we're talking about launch night. This night is all about image. How you look, dress and present yourself is important because you will be judged on everything except your martial arts skills. You and your team need to look dapper. You should be clean-shaven or trimmed, with your teeth brushed and your hair combed. You should be wearing deodorant and your feet should be clean. Instructors should stand out from everybody else with pressed, clean uniforms and their belts on. If you are professional, arrive early and are helpful, people will automatically assume you're good at martial arts too.

Everything I'm going to outline in this section is exactly what we do at all of our new school launches. Most of it can be replicated exactly, regardless of style, with just a few adaptations in techniques.

Setup and welcome

First off, you should arrive half an hour before everyone else to make sure everything is set up properly. This is important for the presentation because you won't just be speaking to the children, but the parents too. Set up a viewing area at the back of the hall where parents can watch the intro class. Obviously, the practical part is for the potential new students, but all the decisions are made by the parents. You've got to make sure they get the information too and that you're checking off all the boxes. Near the viewing area, there should be a table set up with information such as flyers and schedules. Set this up in such a way that people can't leave without going past it, and have an admin present.

Keep in mind that group intros will be back-to-back, so you need to consider that new intros will be arriving towards the end of the previous ones. Make sure you are able to control this when it happens. You don't want people walking in when you're trying to finish up another group.

When the instructor leads the class, they should stand at the front of the class looking toward the viewing area. The students will face the instructor. It is important that this is the positioning you use, to avoid any distractions. You don't want them looking out of windows or doors.

As people come in, greet them by shaking hands. High five the kids or give them a fist bump. Some form of appropriate touch is important for bonding. Everyone should have and wear name tags, so you know exactly who's there, and use people's names when speaking to them.

The class

Once everyone has arrived and been seated, welcome them and give a quick overview of your organisation and, briefly, the specific programme they have come for. Remember not to speak for too long because the children will get bored.

Next, after they've taken their shoes and socks off, have the children line up in height order. Then, one at a time, starting at the back, get them to bow and shout their names so that everyone can hear. Give them a high five and tell them to run one at a time with a sense of urgency to another instructor standing at the front of the line. Give them the command, 'Go!' When they run to the other instructor, he or she will put them into a relaxed position, standing with legs apart and hands behind their back. This is the position used at the start of class. That instructor then takes a step to the side, gives a nod and you send the next one in. Repeat this process until every child is where they need to be. Don't just tell them to line up and expect them to do it, especially the youngest group. You need to space the children out equally and make sure the process is controlled. It can be a bit time-consuming, but it is worth it because it looks impressive.

From there, walk to the front of the class. All the students should be facing you and so should all of the parents sitting at the back. You then begin the first two important lessons of the day. Show them how to come to attention. This is done with their heads held high to demonstrate self-control. When you learn to control your body, you learn to control your emotions and your temper, so we teach this lesson first. We then bow and explain that this shows respect.

For the small children, you might get the pads out and do a coordination game or a balance drill. Keep control of the class at all times, breaking it down into smaller groups if you have the help. If not, that's fine. Do the best you can. The important thing is to keep control of the kids. Keep demonstrating control and respect, repeating your instructions loud enough so the parents can hear them too. Make sure the kids shout out 'yes sir' or 'yes ma'am' in response to all questions asked and that you have total control over the group.

Once you've shown them a jab, a reverse punch, and left and right stance, that's all of the martial arts they will learn in this session but do it on pads and make it into a high-energy drill of some type. We don't do any kicks on the launch night. This lesson is about demonstrating the structure of the classes and showing the parents that they have a sense of urgency and can stand and sit still. There is not enough time for a proper warm-up and you just want to conduct a fifteen-minute practical session. Explain to the parents that it is slower paced than normal and only a demo to see how the children respond to the discipline and structure.

Finish with something fun. With the Cadets or older children you could do some press-ups or sit-ups. Show them how to do the exercises properly and talk about fitness and why it's important. When the class is finished, have them bow and give them a round of applause. Instruct them to sit down next to their parents.

After the class

Once they are seated, you go into more detail about the schedule and costs. You've got to be direct. You can't fluff over things. You need to let them know the days and times of the classes. You must also let them know the price, both per class and monthly. Explain what the joining fee is and that it is a one-time charge.

You also need a call to action that will create a sense of urgency and encourage them to sign up that night, for example a special offer for the first twenty sign-ups. You can repeat this in your confirmation text. The joining fees are elevated so you can give quite a big discount for that evening only, which will encourage enrolment.

End with a recap. Reiterate the prices and the class schedule as well as anything else they need to know. Exceed their expectations. Explain what the grading fees are and let them know they'll need to buy kit in a few months as well as pay licensing fees. If they know everything upfront, they won't mind. You're not going to put them off, but if you leave this information out and they are surprised by it further down the road, you're going to lose people. Give them all the information upfront.

Finally, thank everyone for coming and ask the children, 'Who wants to join?' They'll raise their hands and then you can say, 'Right guys, that's great. We'd love to have you on board. Ask your mum and dad and we'll be over at the table. Put your hand up if you'd like a form to sign.' If you've done a good intro, hands will go up. As soon as one or two hands are in the air, others will follow suit. This is when you hand out the pre-filled or half-filled forms, pens and clipboards so the parents can fill in their Direct Debit forms. You can measure them for suits on launch night too, but wait a month before distributing them to see who sticks with it.

If you sent your confirmation text the day before the launch, then everyone should be primed to buy on launch night and they would have been told to bring a method of payment. Sometimes people will say, 'I haven't got a bank card on me.' If they haven't got a method of payment, get them to fill in the form and sign it by saying, 'We have over twenty people joining tonight on the special offer, but if you sign and fill in your form now, I will text you later for your bank details and I'll still be able to get you in on the offer.'

You can do the same thing for people who say they need to speak with their partners first. Just get them to fill in and sign the form to lock in the offer, and say that you will call or text them later to confirm. If everything's OK, that's great. If not, you can rip it up and they aren't committed, but this way they get the special offer that night.

Anyone who didn't show up can be contacted and rebooked for another time.

After launch night

Once you've got your list of sign-ups, confirm everybody by sending them a confirmation text or email the next day. This should say something like: 'Welcome to the group. We look forward to your first proper class.'

For their first proper class, make sure you've got some sort of starter pack ready. It should include a welcome letter along with a price list for all the equipment they will need to buy, when gradings are and anything else they will need to know.

My martial arts and teaching journey

I trained in martial arts from the age of seven, at a local jiu-jitsu class and some other classes that were held in the local school halls. Around age twelve I started taking it more seriously at the local kung fu club, fighting in a few competitions. Joining English Contact Karate Association (ECKA) at fifteen was a bit of a turning point for me. I won the nationals in points and full contact on the same day at sixteen, then went to Holland and fought in the WKA World Championships, winning the junior section. It was then that things took a turn and I knew I would be doing this for the rest of my life.

I joined the military at eighteen and, for the first few years, I was just doing bits and bobs with martial arts training whenever I could. It was difficult to do anything regularly as we were all over the world. I joined a full-contact club down in Dover when I was based there with 3 Para; I was able to do some good hard training there and get in some fights on the mats and in the ring.

I'd been reading martial arts magazines since I was a kid, and I read about a family called the Winspers, from Kidderminster. Matt and James were brothers, and their dad was Steve. I decided I wanted to train with them. They operated in Halesowen and Kidderminster at the time and a few other places in the West Midlands, UK. I'm from a town nearby called Telford but was based in Dover at the time. The six-hour drive from Dover on Friday afternoons was worth it to me. I would then go home to Telford for the weekend, fight on Sundays and head back to Dover late Sunday evening.

When I started training with the Winspers and Team SMAF, I was blown away by their level of skill. I thought I was pretty good. I'd done a fair number of competitions – well, I thought I had, until I started knocking around with these guys, who'd literally been at it every weekend since they were kids. I learned so much. I couldn't touch either of them and they could hit me with anything they wanted to. That might put some people off, but for me it was amazing. It opened up new possibilities for how good a person could be. I think I was suffering, looking back now, from the Dunning-Kruger effect, where a lack of experience makes someone think they are better than they are at something.[7] You develop a certain amount of skill at the amateur level and you don't realise how much better you could be. You assume the gap isn't that wide. The reality was soon shown to me when I started training with these guys.

I actually did my black belt with them in my early twenties. On the weekend of my test, I had hardly slept for five days because I was on a field exercise while on my junior NCO Cadre with the army. I did my black belt test while still on the course – I had to drive to get my black belt and then go back and finish my course. A pretty intense time.

It was Steve Winsper, their dad, who suggested I begin teaching, which I did in the early 2000s, when I was in my mid-twenties. Things were really kicking off then and people were starting to teach martial arts as a profession, which was unheard of before.

---

7   J Kruger and D Dunning, 'Unskilled and unaware of it: How difficulties in recognizing one's own incompetence lead to inflated self-assessments', *Journal of Personality and Social Psychology*, 77/6 (1999), 1121–1134, https://doi.org/10.1037/0022-3514.77.6.1121

RELAUNCH (GREEN ON 'GO')

Team SMAF. Left to right: James Jordan, Helen Postle, Mark Lester, Linval James, James Winsper, Lee, Ricky Dubidat and James Boyle

Some of the SMAF team at the Ed Byrnes Battle of the Celts tournament

ELITE MARTIAL ARTS INSTRUCTOR

Lee aged fifteen in his house in Brookside, Telford

Lee at the WKA World Championships in Holland in the early '90s, winning the juniors section

ELITE MARTIAL ARTS INSTRUCTOR

Lee aged eighteen passing phase one training (Para Reg), looking like a boy but not feeling like one

RELAUNCH (GREEN ON 'GO')

Lee on operation in Kosovo in 1999

Lee and his brother as a young Second Lieutenant in 1 Para. His brother reached the rank of Captain and was awarded the Military Cross by the Queen. His career was cut short when he was unfortunately run over the day after returning from Iraq, suffering compounded fractures in both legs.

To start with, I taught classes once a week. I loved it. I knew I needed fifty students to be earning as much as I would in the army. I had three months to figure it out before the army stopped paying me. At the end of the three months, I had about 150 students, way over what I needed. I'd had no choice but to make it work as I had a young child and had just bought my first house.

The only reason I started teaching was to do what I loved. I didn't care about the money. As long as I could make the same as when I was in the army, and I could fight whenever I wanted to, I was happy. Teaching was a means to an end. I enjoyed it, but I only wanted enough to pay the bills at this point.

I had never thought about success in business. That didn't happen until later, when I met people like Leigh Childs, John Jepson and Gerard Turvey from Nest Management, who opened my eyes to what could be achieved. These guys were teaching thousands of students in hundreds of locations. It was mind-blowing.

I remember Leigh Childs saying, 'Who wants to be an average instructor and earn an average wage?' At the time, I was thinking I'd be happy enough to be average and have enough students to pay the bills. I had grown up with no money at all and sometimes couldn't even get to school if we couldn't jump-start the car in the morning, unless we found just enough small change down the side of the sofa to catch the bus. I would have been grateful just to be average rather than below average. But when Leigh asked me, 'Why would you want to be average? If you aim for average, that's all you're going to be. Why don't you want to be the best?' I realised that was what I did in all other areas of my life, so why not in business? Because I had never had money before, I had limited what I thought I was capable of. I let go of that mindset, aimed high and went for it.

Summary

In this round, we've covered the importance of having a positive mindset and how to weed out negativity, why 'balance' isn't something you should strive for in your business and how to execute your plan, even in the face of things going wrong (which they will), to ensure you have a successful launch night. At this point, you should be ready and raring to go.

In this first part of the book, we have gone through the steps to establish your martial arts business; we are now ready to move on to Part Two, Make It Great, starting with Round 3.

PART TWO
MAKE IT GREAT

Once you have launched or relaunched your school, you need to know how to build it and sustain its success over time. In this part of the book, you will learn how to create a business that will be around for a long time and how to ensure it will thrive so that it can support you and your family for many years to come, without burying you in work.

ROUND 3
Rapid Growth (Advance To Battle)

This round covers everything you need to do once you have launched or relaunched your school successfully. Your objective now is rapid growth in the early stage, so you can build it into a large, successful school. The military analogy for this stage is 'Advance to battle', as you are now moving towards your main objective.

As a paratrooper, once you have completed the jump and landed safely, you need to complete a quick check of your equipment to make sure you still have everything and that it is in working order. You look around to see where everyone is, pick up your equipment and advance to the RV (rendezvous). This is the spot you are told to meet at once you land, so you can gain strength as a group. Once you are at the RV, all of your section, then the platoon and then the company will be checked in to establish if anyone is missing and/or if there are casualties. In peacetime, everyone will be accounted for. If it was operational, in reality they would gather as many men as could be found, as quickly as possible, to have enough to complete the mission. Then they would head off, regardless of casualties and people unaccounted for. Momentum can't be lost. Mission success is the priority.

Once the group is checked off and formed up, you must advance to your objective and 'battle'. That could be to fight, hold a position, or provide extra numbers for troops already on the ground. Whatever it is, you won't have landed directly on the objective and will need to progress there on foot.

Once you have completed your preparation for your school launch ('Red on') and have successfully opened with a big launch ('Green on "go"'), you will advance to the rapid growth phase of your business, and your objective is to win: a successful martial arts school that supports you and your family and services your students to the best of your ability. Use the momentum of all this positive energy and the excited new students and parents to grow the school as quickly as you can. No school just keeps getting bigger and bigger. The majority of schools will grow the most after the launch and in the first six months to a year. After this, they normally level off. They can still grow, but at a much slower rate. People will start to drop off and there are seasonal variations, which means you will get a bigger drop-off at certain times of the year like Christmas and summer holidays. There will come a point where more growth is possible, but the amount of effort required would be better spent opening up more locations.

My fighting experience and how I raised my game

After I began teaching, I continued with my fighting and went further down the points fighting side of things. I had been training with some amazing fighters, the Winspers and Team SMAF, who I suppose were a little more 'old school' than what you see in tournaments today. These were tough, hard men with great physical abilities and who could hit hard. The training wasn't just points, though, it was light contact and full contact. It was as hard as anything I had ever done.

I then started training with different types of fighters, to open up my horizons, Sam Timmis being one of them. He was just seventeen when I met him. We sparred once or twice a week for a few years, and it was training with him that took my fighting to the next level. He had a different style that made me think. I didn't learn to move backward when fighting until I started training with him – I would just attack. He slowed me down and made me more intelligent with both my attacks and defences – I had to be, or I couldn't hit him with anything clean. He was a successful fighter and won many titles.

WAKO GB team

As my fighting progressed, I started to beat the more seasoned fighters and people I'd looked up to for years, eventually winning my first WAKO (World Association of Kickboxing Organisations) British title. This was a big deal for me at the time, as the standard was unbelievable in my heavyweight class. You had to win this to get selected to go to squad training, where the main GB team would be picked. Sometimes, even if you won, you still had to fight off with other fighters who had been placed, so that they could be sure they were bringing the very best from the UK to the world or European championships.

It's obviously a great honour to fight for your country at such a prestigious event. I had never seen anything like it. Every fighter was the champion of their county and had worked their way up through the ranks. They now have a WAKO World Championship for the under eighteens and the standard that these kids compete at is unbelievable. Every fight is like a final, with the fighters battling it out with close scores and so much pressure. I loved the variables, all the different things you could do to make little differences. Anyone who has been and fought for their country in combat sports will know the feeling of camaraderie built through shared hardship and a fight against a common perceived enemy. It's not dissimilar to being in the military. Even the guys I wasn't that friendly with back in the day while we were fighting, when we meet now we can reflect on the strong bond that only a fighter understands.

Hierarchy of values

The hierarchy of values is a concept developed by Myres McDougal, which comprises of a list of values arranged by importance.[8] This is a helpful concept if you want to be successful in growing your school, as you can use it make sure that you are directing your attention towards the most important areas of your life. Let me explain.

---

8   MS McDougal and HD Lasswell, *Jurisprudence for a Free Society* (Martinus Nijhoff Publishers, 1992)

The poor man with no money looks at the rich man with the nice car and the big house and a different partner every time he sees him and thinks to himself, 'I wish I was as successful as him.' The rich man looks at the poor man with his wife and two children and thinks, 'I wish I had a family like his.'

The truth is that the 'rich' man is recently divorced and has estranged children who want nothing to do with him. The 'poor' man sees his children every day, he takes them to school and to their different clubs and has a close and loving relationship with his wife.

Which of these men is the most successful? In reality, each of them puts their time and effort into the things in their lives that hold the highest value to them.

Everyone has a hierarchy of values. Whatever they place the most value on, they will succeed in. People are successful at whatever is at the top of their hierarchy of values. If you are an athlete, you'll make sure that you train every day and your diet is on point, no matter what else is happening in your life. If you value nice clothes, cars and going out a lot, you will always find money for these things first over everything else. If family or work are what's at the top, then you will spend more time and put more effort into these areas. Equally, though, if you're a drug addict or gambler, what you place more value on than anything else is getting your next hit or finding a casino.

You look around at the world and judge everyone, including yourself, by the typical Western ideas of success, when in fact you are already successful in whatever tops your values list. But this might not be what you *want* to be successful in, as most people are totally unconscious of what is at the top of their values hierarchy until they look carefully.

If you're not where you want to be at the moment, write down what is most important to you and make sure that this is what your time, effort and money are directed towards. Because if you're not where you want to be, then your conscious values are not in line with your unconscious values.

Take advantage of laziness

People are lazy. We are designed to be this way, to conserve energy and calories. It makes sense. If you lived in a time when resources were scarce and you were expending energy on things unnecessarily, then you might not survive. If you watch people as I do, you will see just how lazy everyone is, including you. It's built into us; you can't escape it.

But once you realise how lazy you are, you can start addressing it – and it's important that you do. You need to become aware of your typical downfalls so you can avoid them, which is necessary if you want to be as efficient as possible in the continued growth and development of yourself and your school.

A while back, I got a new sofa and table in my living room. I noticed when I was having a glass or two of wine at the weekend that the position of the new sofa meant that I was seated a bit further back than I was previously, and the table was in a different position. This meant I had to push myself up first and then reach out and pick up my wine to take a sip. With the old set up, I could just put my hand out and grab it. Because of this change, I noticed that I drank half the amount of wine that I did before (even I'm lazy, apparently). I was shocked, surprised and fascinated by this. Because I had to do something that took effort in order to have a sip of wine, I did it less. I decided to buy a new table that I could get to easier, but this taught me a valuable lesson about people. If you make something difficult, fewer people will do it, or they'll do it less; conversely, if you make it easy, they'll do it more.

All big businesses know this and will do opt-outs and free trials where you need to physically go back and do something laborious to avoid becoming a member. They rely on your laziness to make money. Now that you understand this, think about how having an opt-in or opt-out system could help with certain processes and decisions in your students' journey. It could be gradings, kit sales, seminars or upgrades. There are things that will help your students' progress and save them from their own laziness – it will also help your ability to organise things. It won't harm your integrity as there will always be an opt-out for anything that isn't suitable or wanted.

Good problems and bad problems

You will always have problems, no matter how rich, famous or successful you become. In fact, typically, the more successful you become, the more problems you will have. I believe P Diddy once said something to this effect.

But as I always tell my team, there are good problems and bad problems. A bad problem is having no students on launch night. A good problem is spending all your time answering messages on Facebook booking intros. Before you start moaning about a 'problem', think about whether it's a good or a bad problem. I want you to have as many good problems in your life as you can possibly deal with. That means you're going to be busy sorting them out and finding solutions to make your situation better. You will have bad problems too. That's just life. You'll need to resolve these as best as you can and try to turn them into positives.

I don't even use the word 'problems' anymore. They are just things that need sorting out – and the more things you get sorted each day, the more successful you will be. Welcome these things that need sorting into your life and change your perspective on them – this is what success looks like. The reason you see 'problems' is because of the way your mind works. Remember that your mind is a survival tool designed to solve problems, so it is always looking for them. It's a tool, so use it – don't let it use you. The mind is a great servant but a terrible master.

External marketing

Marketing is fundamental to success and so is a main focus of the rapid growth stage. There are many different types of marketing you can utilise.

Traditional marketing

Most people are familiar with traditional forms of marketing like posters, flyers, newspapers and magazine ads. When I first started, these were the main ways to get your message out. A lot of these still work and should not be forgotten. Posters at your locations and local shops are effective. Ads in free local magazines are also beneficial, but to get the best value, buy a small ad and agree to have accompanying editorial and pictures. Do this before you book so that you have leverage, as they want to sell the space. I don't use newspaper advertising much now, unless it's a free article when we have done something in the community or, more importantly, one of the students has. This is the best way to use newspapers. Flyers also work well, but I don't send them out in newspapers anymore. Instead, I distribute them directly at an assembly or event.

Social media

Social media has become the primary channel for disseminating information to a vast audience. It allows you to target and select specific groups, ensuring that your message reaches the right people. This includes targeting those who have previously engaged with your ads or pages. It's crucial to communicate a clear offering and identify your target audience. Additionally, incorporating a compelling call to action is essential to prompt immediate contact.

Focus on emphasising the benefits for the individual or their children, rather than personal achievements, awards, or the style you teach. Using fresh images for each ad campaign is important to maintain a sense of novelty, especially since you'll be displaying ads to similar audiences periodically. Mastering this aspect of marketing is an art form.

Allocate a monthly budget for your social media advertising and ensure that each ad presents a unique and attractive offer tailored to the season and target audience. Consistently post on your page at least three times a week, incorporating pictures and videos to help visitors get a sense of your club's atmosphere and personality.

Although entire books have been written about leveraging social media, the key takeaway is that it is an invaluable marketing tool for generating consistent leads. Combine its power with other methods mentioned here for optimal results. Facebook and Instagram have proven to be the most effective platforms, while others have successfully employed TikTok. Utilise efficient strategies to achieve the best results with minimal effort. For example, advertising on Facebook can be linked to your Instagram page, so one paid ad is distributed across both platforms.

Pursuing efficiency is not laziness; it's adhering to the 80/20 rule. There may be more intricate ways to accomplish the tasks described, but the additional cost and effort may yield only marginally improved results. Focus on maximising effectiveness with the least amount of effort.

SEO

Search engine optimisation (SEO) is an important aspect of online marketing and helps to ensure that your website and social media pages rank highly on Google search results by optimising your content and keywords. You should incorporate relevant wording and content on your platforms to improve visibility. When creating your website, the developers or copywriters should use relevant keywords and phrases that will be recognised by Google and displayed to local users searching for your services. While SEO is cost-effective, it does have its drawbacks.

One downside of SEO is that it takes time to yield results, as you'll be competing with other businesses. If your competitors have been around longer than you, reaching the top of search results can be a challenging and time-consuming endeavour. Despite these challenges, SEO remains an essential aspect of online marketing that should not be overlooked.

Google Maps and Google My Business listings

Leveraging Google Maps and Google My Business (GMB) listings is a cost-effective way to boost your online presence. These listings usually appear before other search results on Google, providing an excellent opportunity for visibility.

Google Maps is a widely used navigation tool that helps users find businesses and services in their local area. By adding your business to Google Maps, you ensure that potential customers can easily locate you. To do this, claim your business listing and provide accurate information, such as your address, phone number and business hours.

Google My Business is a platform that enables you to manage your online presence across Google, including Search and Maps. Creating and optimising your GMB listing is crucial for local search success. To get started, claim your business and verify your listing. Ensure that your business information is accurate and up to date, including contact details, website and hours of operation. You should regularly update your listing with new photos, promotions and events to keep it fresh and engaging.

It is a great idea to encourage satisfied customers to leave reviews on your GMB listing, as positive reviews improve your credibility and search ranking. Respond to reviews, both positive and negative, to show your commitment to customer satisfaction.

Despite being free resources, many businesses overlook the benefits of Google Maps and Google My Business listings. Make the most of these tools to increase your visibility and stay ahead of the competition.

Google PPC advertising

Depending on your location, Google Pay-Per-Click (PPC) can be an effective method of generating leads. Before investing in PPC, ensure that your website is well designed and features a booking form to facilitate direct bookings. Optimise your site's SEO to improve its organic search ranking – this is particularly important for smaller towns and villages where traffic is lower. For businesses in larger cities, and especially for full-time locations or schools in more competitive areas, utilising PPC can be a strategic way to secure a prominent position on search result pages.

The way that Google PPC works is that you bid on keywords relevant to your business and you only pay when users click on your ad. This form of advertising helps you reach potential customers who are *actively searching* for services like yours.

If you decide to use it, allocate a monthly budget for PPC campaigns. Carefully select your target keywords and monitor the performance of your ads. Continuously optimise your campaigns to maximise your return on investment and stay ahead of the competition. By combining PPC with organic SEO efforts, you can improve your online presence and attract a steady stream of leads.

Marketing funnels

Marketing funnels, including sales and lead funnels, are becoming indispensable tools in various industries. Although they are not yet widely adopted in certain sectors, their effectiveness is proven in other niches.

This approach is based on the idea that customers can be divided into two categories: those who are ready to buy (5%) and those who are either unaware of your offerings or unsure of their needs (95%). You then create tailored marketing funnels to target each group more effectively.

For the ready-to-buy 5%, your ad strategies should be more focused and sales-oriented. Utilise a funnel to guide these highly interested leads towards purchasing or taking advantage of your offer. Although the process is too detailed to cover here, combining a well-crafted direct-response ad campaign with this type of funnel can help you filter out unproductive leads and increase attendance for trial classes.

For the 95% who are either unaware or undecided, you should employ lead magnets to capture their attention. Offer free gifts in exchange for their contact information, enabling you to follow up with offers and keep them engaged. The lead magnet should educate prospects about your brand and help build their confidence in you.

Provide additional value through free content such as booklets, scorecards, questionnaires, brochures, instructional videos or links to relevant blog posts. By targeting this larger, less competitive market segment, you can expand your potential customer base while your competitors focus on the 5% who are ready to buy.

Using marketing funnels for lead generation yields highly qualified leads who have a clear understanding of your offerings and recognise that you are the right choice for them. Automation tools, like Active Campaign or Klaviyo, can help manage automated email campaigns for nurturing these leads. Once you have prepared your free gifts, pre-written emails and offers with links, you should see a steady stream of leads.

Although setting up these funnels requires some initial effort, they foster trust, brand awareness and high-quality leads in the long run. Invest time in nurturing these relationships to reap the benefits of your marketing funnels.

AI and ChatGPT

Artificial intelligence (AI) is a revolutionary technology that is transforming the way businesses operate. ChatGPT is an advanced AI language model that has the ability to understand natural language and generate human-like responses. It is an exciting development that martial arts school owners can utilise to enhance their marketing strategies. You can use ChatGPT to create a more personalised experience for potential students and automate your marketing campaigns, saving time and resources. ChatGPT can also help schools generate leads, increase conversions and, ultimately, grow their businesses.

It's important to establish guidelines for your school's use of ChatGPT to ensure that the content generated aligns with your brand and values. This means providing clear prompts and context for the AI to work with, so it understands the brand's tone of voice and messaging. It's also important to review the content generated by ChatGPT to ensure it is appropriate and aligned with the school's values. Consistency is key, and ChatGPT can help you to maintain a consistent voice for your school across all marketing channels.

As with any technology, AI comes with its own terminology that may be unfamiliar to those new to the field. Understanding this is important for effective communication and collaboration. Some key terms to get to grips with are natural language processing (NLP), machine learning, neural networks and deep learning. By understanding these terms and concepts, you can better understand the capabilities and limitations of ChatGPT and how to leverage its power to enhance your marketing efforts.

Before diving into using ChatGPT, it's important to have a solid understanding of the fundamentals of marketing. This includes identifying your target audiences, crafting effective messaging and designing high-converting landing pages. Once you understand these key concepts, you can use ChatGPT to its full potential and create effective marketing campaigns for your school that will resonate with potential students.

The success you'll have with using AI for marketing depends largely on the quality of the prompts you provide as input. To ensure the best results, you need to know how to craft effective prompts that give enough context and information for ChatGPT to generate accurate, relevant and high-quality content. Context and prompt engineering are key aspects of using ChatGPT; the more it knows about the school's brand, audience and offers, the better the results will be.

Free face-to-face marketing

This is my favourite type of marketing because it's effective and free. But it's a dying art, mainly because it takes a lot of effort. The first 10–15 years of my business growth was driven solely by these methods. It is the fundamental building block of my organisation.

School visits

As a martial arts instructor, you are a key person within your local community and well placed to help the local children. It's important that you position yourself like this with the schools and build up a good relationship with all of them. When you have been doing this for a few years, they will be calling and asking you to come in for PE classes, sports days, parents' evenings, summer fetes, antibullying initiatives or healthy eating week. Whatever the reason, you should always take the opportunity to be there.

If it's a summer fete, you can get a gazebo, a table with flyers and a pull-up banner. If you have students who go to that school, ask them to meet you there in uniform. If not, then just pick children who walk past to work with you to practise, then book them for a free trial.

Take note if any of the mums or dads from your club work at one of the primary schools or are in the PTA (parent teacher association), as they will know who to ask to get you in the schools. Another good way of working with the schools is by asking the children who already go to your classes. They will all go to a local school. Get them to speak to the school about you coming in. If you give out a 'student of the month award', ask the winner – or, even better, ask their mum or dad. They will be super motivated to see their child at a school assembly and will know how to make it happen. You can also see if you can present belts to your students at school.

Primary school assemblies

I can't emphasise enough how effective promotional primary school assemblies are, if they are done in the way I outlined in Round 1. With these, you must understand that your entire purpose is to drive intros to your school and take bookings for intro classes.

Town centres/high streets

Any opportunity you have to get yourself in front of the general public, take it. We are often found on the local high streets or town centres with a pull-up banner, table, flyers, a set of focus pads and a few mats. We will be in uniform and have at least a few children in full uniform with us to give out the flyers. We'll be armed with clipboards, with the sole purpose of signing up as many people as possible for a free trial class the following week. Rather than just standing there, we will sometimes run a competition to give away a free suit or gloves and ask the local children if they want to take part. We normally get them to do something easy on the pads, like throw as many punches as they can in ten seconds. We then tell them that because they participated, they will get a free class and give them an appointment card.

Sometimes we do things on a bigger scale. If you follow us on social media, you will have seen some of the demos we put on, which are an even better way of getting attention. The big demos are normally held over the weekend – we move all the Saturday morning classes to the town centre. The kids and parents love it and tell all their friends. It can create a big crowd. We will sometimes have one of the instructors or students dressed up as a superhero or a character. This breaks people's patterns, so they stop and look. The children obviously love it. We accompany this with a great offer for people signing up that day. We can get twenty to thirty sign-ups on a good day, with the right people on the ground – and we're talking about new members here, not leads.

Swimming lessons

If you have a local sports centre with swimming lessons, the viewing area there is a great place to put up a pull-up banner. Take some flyers and start booking people. Swimming lessons normally last thirty minutes so you'll see lots of parents and children throughout the course of the evening. We have had instructors get over fifty leads in just a few hours.

All of the methods I have explained in this section are the best ways to get new leads, because you are face-to-face with the parents and children. They can see what you're doing and feel your energy. They are not easy to book though. You need to be resourceful and persistent. Think outside the box and find out through your network who works at these places, as it is always easier to get access when you're referred.

Internal marketing

Internal marketing is marketing that you can do in your classes. These methods are normally free, or with minimal printing fees.

All internal marketing communications can be texted and emailed to current students as well as posted in your student Facebook groups, pages or WhatsApp groups. I would still suggest making a flyer and getting one into every student's hands, put it up on the notice board too, if you have one. Some of the internal promotional events and initiatives you can run are detailed below.

Buddy days

Invite students to bring in a friend for a pre-arranged class. Use themes so you can have different ones depending on the time of the year. Popular ones are days to bring friends, siblings, mums for Mother's Day, dads for Father's Day, women and girls for International Women's Day, etc. You can also have Christmas parties or summer BBQs that you charge for, but that are free or discounted for those who bring a friend. At all these events, make sure that you collect all of the friends' contact details so that you can get in touch with a special offer after the event.

Referral competitions

This is when you actively encourage your students to bring friends to class in order to get a prize. As with any type of marketing, how the message is delivered is important to the level of buy-in you can generate. It's a good idea to have a deadline and offer a reward for the top referrers. The best students for bringing in referrals are always your new students. They are keen and just need to be asked. Some schools give particularly good prizes as motivation, but it works just as well if you give away a free month, or a set of gloves, a T-shirt that you can't buy or badges. I know some schools that are hardcore with their referrals and make it part of their first belt, where students must refer a friend to show their commitment to the school. If you don't ask, you don't get.

We normally make up a VIP card and give every student a set amount, so they have value. You can put these in new students' starter packs and run this initiative on an ongoing basis, or do seasonal competitions and give them to everyone at your school in one go. They need to have your school logo and address with 'free class' written on there, plus somewhere on the card for the referring student to put their name so that the referral can be tracked. Once a student has handed out all their cards, you can issue them new ones. Track the top referrers with a chart or scoreboard so that people can see who is in the lead. Remember, children are competitive; seeing who is currently winning is a reward in itself and also makes the rest try harder.

Win a year free

I run this competition when I move my classes into full-time centres, but they can be done anytime. We do it as a referral competition and put everyone who is referred into a draw for a big prize. This competition can only run for two to three weeks, as you need a winner and the leads will go cold if left too long. You can give your students flyers with a bit to cut out for their friend's details, and can advertise the competition in the local papers and on social media. The first prize is one year of free martial arts training, but we also have many other prizes like free uniforms, free gloves, free T-shirts, free private lessons and free gradings.

Make sure that you get all your students involved by getting as many friends and family as possible to enter the competition. We allow all students to put in one entry for themselves for every friend they enter. You will also get people entering from your social media and newspaper advertising, who may not know anyone from the club.

On all the entry forms, you should ask people to write the reason they think they should win. From all of the entries, you pick one winner – the person who you feel is the most deserving. You should pick a non-member for the main prize of one year's free training, all the others can be picked at random from your existing students who worked hard bringing in the referrals. This competition doesn't cost you a huge amount, as you can buy the physical prizes wholesale and the free year costs you nothing. In my experience, the winner normally signs up after the year is over if they are still training. In addition, you'll have the details of loads of people who are interested in martial arts classes.

Make sure that everyone else who entered the competition gets a 'third prize' of two weeks' free classes. When you contact them, make sure you tell them that they have 'won the third prize', as then you'll have excited prospects coming in. You know what you need to do with them once they are at the school.

Follow the students

If you have opened multiple locations, then once the dust has settled and things have levelled off, look at which locations are strongest. You will always get an imbalance; there will be some locations that are packed every week and you just can't fit in any more students, others will be a bit more challenging. The first thing to do is turn your attention to the weaker areas and try and boost these schools. If that brings them up to the level of the others, great. If not, then make a logical decision. If you have an instructor running ten locations and two of these are packed and two of these are quiet, close the quiet ones and run more classes at the busiest ones. Or open at two new locations.

I make sure we maximise the full potential of our instructors. I see a lot of instructors with a handful of students and not able to get their location off the ground. The instructor is obviously going to be connected to the students and not want to let them down, but if it is taking too much effort to grow a location, it is better to redirect that effort into starting a new one. Your busiest and biggest locations will be the ones that become your full-time locations. You are basically testing the market before you decide where to base yourself, while also building up income and students so that when you do make the move to full-time, you can use the money you turn over to support the project rather than using savings or having to borrow money.

If you have a full-time centre already, look at the classes that get the most students and put on more of these. If you don't have enough space in your timetable, close the classes that have the fewest attendees. You must follow the students, not your own agenda or what you think is easiest.

Change your mindset and the world changes with it

By the time I was in my mid-twenties, I had been away on two operational tours and visited many different countries, I had already met more people and had more experiences than most people would in two lifetimes. I had made myself into what I thought I needed to be in order to be safe in the world. But in all honesty, I had created a monster. I had built walls around my mind so that nothing and no one could penetrate it or hurt me emotionally. Because of this, I was emotionally unavailable to those close to me. I would regularly be in confrontations and fights, sometimes daily. I had anger issues and my fuse was not so much short as non-existent. I would go from normal to extreme anger and violence in a split second, with no warning for the people around me. I thought I was happy, because in my eyes I was successful and was able to get the job done with anything I put my mind to.

But on reflection, I was still scared and was acting this way as a defence mechanism. Due to my dyslexia, I couldn't read or write very well when I left the army at twenty-six, though I soon learned when I started reading self-development books. In reading I had once again found something that could facilitate self-improvement, and was soon addicted to it (I was later diagnosed with obsessive compulsive disorder). I read over 200 books on subjects that I believed could help me, and learned to read and write properly along the way.

On this journey of self-development, I realised that I was subconsciously bringing all of the violence and confrontation into my life myself, through my own behaviour, due to unconscious fear. As soon as I realised that I was the issue, I changed overnight – and my whole world changed too. I must have been giving off certain vibes that people with similar issues were picking up on and we were acting out our expectations of the world with each other. I realised that the more fights and confrontations I got into, the weaker and more paranoid I was becoming. It was not making me stronger. I expected and was ready for trouble, so I found it everywhere I turned.

Once I recognised this, I stopped looking for confrontations and the trouble just wasn't there anymore. I moved areas, started going to different places and spent time with different friends. All of a sudden, I occupied a different world and could be a different person, the person I wanted to be.

It was then that I started going down a spiritual route, which seems to happen to a lot of people once they start to improve themselves. I remember hearing that anger was the 'bodyguard of sadness' and thinking, 'Well, I'm not sad.' As far as I was concerned, I was one of the happiest people I knew. I always managed to get what I wanted somehow, and I had attained a level of external success. It was a massive epiphany for me when I realised that the way I was actually feeling from moment to moment, my internal reality, was not pleasant – far from it. Just because my external world was in order, it didn't mean I was.

I then became consumed, over the course of around five years in my early to mid-thirties, by some intense spiritual soul-searching. I was obsessively reading and meditating for hours every day. Everything I read or watched on TV was in some way linked to this effort. I contacted and met with people I had read about or spiritual teachers I had seen on TV. I went on retreats, trying to unpack things and go as deep into myself as I could. From the outside, it seemed to my wife that I was losing my mind, but for me, it felt like I was only just starting to understand myself. She thought I was having a breakdown and worried for my sanity.

During this time, I started, out of nowhere, to have panic attacks and nightmares every night. This lasted a couple of years. Cracks had started to appear in what I thought was an impenetrable exterior. The false character and ego I had built up had stopped protecting me and it was too much for my mind to cope with. Looking back now, I must have seemed insane. Without going into too much detail, I had what some people would call a spiritual awakening and others might call a breakdown. I'm not too sure myself what it was, but my life changed dramatically from then. My mind had worked itself up into a frenzy and then just surrendered. I went from being totally neurotic and paranoid to feeling totally peaceful and at ease with everything. I think my mind had just returned to its normal state, like when you're a child, without the big ego and adult problems. My OCD pretty much disappeared and my relationship with alcohol and partying, which had been getting increasingly out of hand, changed as I no longer needed these things to stop the screaming in my skull – this had mostly stopped.

Things levelled off, but it took a couple of years of flip-flopping back and forth. When I was thirty-five, I decided to stop fighting, as it didn't have the same meaning to me anymore. I had changed quite considerably during that time and was in a more stable and truthful place in my own mind. I felt as though I had recalibrated and lost a big part of my ego. I think this happens to a lot of people as they get older; for me, it just happened earlier and over a short time period.

Summary

In Round 3, we have gone over exactly what to do to harness the momentum of your launch and the early excitement of the students and parents to build your school up to the next level. I've gone over the different types of marketing, both free and paid, that you can use to get as many leads as possible for your school, including AI, a powerful tool that you can leverage to create personalised and effective marketing content, generate leads, increase conversions and, ultimately, grow your businesses.

In the next round we will cover retention (The Battle) and discuss the best way to train all your students to get them to the highest standard, and how to retain them for as long as possible. We will also go over how to run the classes along with the dojo management side of things.

ROUND 4
Retention (The Battle)

In this round, we will cover retention – how to keep hold of your students once you have them and maintain the success you have built up. The military analogy for this round is 'The battle'. Any successful school owner will tell you that growing your school is only half of the work; the main battle is maintaining a high level of success. This is achieved by creating strong and effective lifelong habits, systems and processes.

You have jumped, landed, met up with the rest of your platoon, advanced to the objective and made it to the start line. But the battle is still to come. Everything you have done so far has been to get you to this point. A paratrooper's main job isn't the jump or getting to the destination. These are just means to an end. The reason you have to be so physically fit and courageous enough to jump from a plane is so that, after all the stress and hard work just to get to that point, you are still able to fight with everything you have. Now the real work starts. This is exactly the same for instructors when they have successfully established their schools. You have built the school up and got it to where it should be and now you need to do your job: service and retain the students to the best of your ability.

I have personally launched over 200 martial arts schools and have signed up thousands of students. Over the years I have noticed that some instructors use the momentum and continue to grow after the launch, while others go backwards. In the system I have developed, we launch over the course of four weeks from 'Green on "go"' and 150–200 new students sign up within this time frame. This system has proven itself in many successful launches.

Once the school is handed over to the instructor, it is their responsibility to keep the momentum going and good habits in place. You need to be a 200-students type instructor with good personal discipline and habits. Your school reflects the type of person you are. If an instructor was just given a full-time centre with 400 students, where they didn't earn them or grow with the school, they wouldn't fully appreciate their value. When this happens, the school starts to decrease in numbers until it settles at a level the instructor is capable of managing with their current mindset and habits.

The same goes for money, relationships and other areas of life. You will have heard, I'm sure, of people who win the lottery and then lose it all. These kinds of things are a reflection of you and the type of person you are. It also works the other way around. There are plenty of stories of millionaires losing everything, then making it back again. This is because of their expectations, work ethic, knowledge and self-worth. I have placed instructors in schools and seen it go both ways. The little things, done correctly and repeatedly, lead to success.

The small things matter

Success isn't one big thing; it's lots of small things done consistently. You build up certain behaviours through consistent attention to your objective. Every action you take either brings you a step closer to or away from success. Improvement is normally slow, but much damage can be done suddenly if you make bad decisions. You can lose all your money, sabotage a lifelong relationship, or ruin the reputation of your company literally overnight. The upside is slow, but the downside can be rapid.

Have a clear goal. It's fine to think a lot about this goal or dream, to fantasise about it in your mind. I've done this with everything I've ever desired since childhood. But you cannot focus only on the goal, or you will get disconnected from the process. You will step out of the moment and into your head and all you will be able to see and feel is the gap between where you want to be and where you are. It's OK to feel this, as it is motivating, but don't live there. It's an uncomfortable place to be.

Know your goal, but then disassociate from it and turn your focus to the process of achieving it and what you can do right now. Take one step at a time. Don't overwhelm yourself by thinking about the long journey ahead. Focus on now.

Fighters can come unstuck with this in tournaments when they think too much about the guy in the final rather than the person in front of them. You won't win if you're in your mind. Submerge yourself in the current fight, focusing on one point or technique at a time. If you execute these right, you will achieve your desired outcome.

In business and in life, the people who seem to have it together consistently make good decisions and turn problems into solutions, having the discipline to do what is right and necessary. This is where you need to be. Over time, this develops into a habit and you start doing it unconsciously; it becomes part of your personality.

Maintain this mindset, with the aim of constant and never-ending improvement, and what you achieve over a year or several years will blow your mind. This is the single most important habit to develop to be elite. You need to stay the course, figuring things out one step at a time. Keep moving forward, taking consistent action and steps towards your goal.

That one additional rep, the bonus training session, the extra section you fought in, the healthy meal you ate when you didn't want to, all of these make a difference. But the training session you skipped, the reps you didn't do and the tournaments missed, all of these make a difference too. It's the mindset of 'I can miss one, it doesn't matter' that needs changing.

It *always* matters. It's not the 'thing' in question that's the issue, it's the mindset, which will creep in more and more, if you let it. There is no easy route to this life. Remember, if you're not doing it, someone else in your industry is and they will take the glory. Keep chipping away. A masterpiece is made one stroke at a time.

Statistics

Bearing all of the above in mind, let's talk about statistics. Statistics let you take a bird's eye view of your business and show you exactly what is going on.

If you were driving a car and you didn't know how fast it was going, how much petrol was in the tank, or what direction it was headed in, you would never get to your destination. It's the same for your business. Knowing the stats helps you to understand exactly where you are, meaning you can figure out how to get to where you want to be and monitor your progress towards that destination.

There are certain stats that are essential to monitor for your school. I have all the instructors that I employ send the key stats to me before lunchtime on Monday mornings. I ask for the following:

- **Student count** – the number of 'live' students that are paying by Direct Debit

- **Active student count** – the number of students that were in classes last week
- **Cancellations** – the number of Direct Debits that were cancelled last week
- **Intros** – the amount that are booked for this week

A school owner should do this every Monday to see what the last week looked like. If it looks bad, you need to see this so that you can sort it out. If there are no intros booked, this will motivate you to take action. If the active students count is low, you should text all students who haven't been training to let them know they have been missed in class and that they can make up their classes another day. Remember, all students are either closer to the black belt or closer to leaving, there are no grey areas. If they haven't been in that week, they are closer to leaving.

Another handy time to collect stats is when you are working out where your leads are coming from. Get a sheet with your advertising and track where each lead came from. If you don't know, then start asking this as part of your booking process. At the end of the month, add up how much you're spending on marketing in each area and divide that by the number of leads and you have your cost per lead. You can do the same with sign-ups to work out the cost per new student acquisition.

Dojo management

There are various aspects to dojo management that need to be carefully considered and consistently practised in order to build and run a successful school. We'll discuss these in the following sections.

Class groups

There are three main age groups that we teach. We split them up this way as each group is totally different and needs to have information delivered in an age-appropriate way to get the best effect.

The first age group is four to seven years. We call these the Little Soldiers, but they are called Little Ninjas or Little Dragons in some schools. Their classes should only be thirty minutes long and broken down into five-minute sections: a five-minute warm-up, a five-minute stretch, three five-minute main themes, and five minutes to cool down. The first five minutes (the warm-up) should be a high-energy game or drill. With every five-minute section, you should change the position of the children, the drill, the instructor, or all of the above. If they are in lines, put them in a queue for the next drill, or in front of a mirror, on a pad, impact shield or bag. Use games and drills to keep them engaged and make sure to use animated examples to explain key concepts. Drop down to their level when addressing them. It doesn't matter what style of martial arts you do; you can use an adapted version that is appropriate for the group. They should also have their own belt system, separate from all the other students.

Our Cadets are age eight to eleven; in other schools, these might be referred to as juniors or the main kids' classes. These classes run off the same syllabus as my adults, but we deliver it in an age-appropriate way, with extra emphasis on discipline, self-control and respect. The classes should be forty-five minutes long and should involve a good level of physical training (PT), as fitness isn't something kids do a lot of these days. Most kids don't even walk to school anymore. PT progression as they go through the belts is important.

We try to create urgency in the dojo. This can be done in the warm-up part of the class quite easily, regardless of what style you teach. I've gone to a lot of martial arts classes in the past where the kids hardly do any warm-up or stretching. Use the first ten minutes of the class to get the kids going, with them shouting out commands and competing against each other to raise the energy level of the class.

With both of the kids' programmes, you need to make sure you are constantly reinforcing boundaries. If something wasn't shouted back loud enough, ask again. If they weren't fast enough, get them to repeat the move. There should be purpose and intention in all their actions.

As students advance, make sure they are split down by ability so that you can do more specific training targeted to their individual needs. Advanced students can double up on classes as they improve. We normally have a sparring class between the advanced Cadets and the adults so the groups can mix. They get to train more, which is fundamental for progress. The beginners are then starting on manageable forty-five-minute classes and the more advanced students will be doing two or even three classes on their chosen night. In my opinion, this is the best way to run things, rather than longer classes for everyone. This also makes it easier to sign people up, as the barrier to entry is low if they are starting on two forty-five-minute classes a week and then building up as they progress. You also get the opportunity to re-educate them on what's needed.

The next class is for those aged twelve and above. These are split into mixed adults and ladies-only. In some of our full-time centres, we have teen classes, but when you first start, stick with the main group categories as these serve the most people to the best standard. There should be separate beginner classes for all new students. These classes should be forty-five minutes long, typically consisting of five minutes of warm-up, ten minutes of exercise, five minutes of stretching, twenty minutes on the main theme, and five minutes of cool down. You can adjust the length of time you spend on each part of the lesson depending on what your lesson plan is, but not the order you do them in. Make sure you start slowly and build up in intensity as the students warm up. There needs to be a good level of fitness training at the start of class. For some people, this is their only exercise. With all classes, make them high energy and fun but challenging. I've been to many schools where students are standing or sitting around doing nothing. You only have forty-five minutes, so make sure you fill every second with activity.

Our ladies-only classes are highly successful. You can target these to focus more on the fitness side of things and less on combat to accommodate this market and the reason they are there. In my experience, after a few months, the women start to gain confidence in the combat element, jump into regular classes and build up to sparring. Cater to what they want, which in most cases I've found is weight loss, fitness and community.

Instructor positioning

As an instructor, make sure that you are marked out as different from the students. We wear black uniforms. When teaching, don't just stand at the front of the room counting out repetitions. Move around from student to student. Stand tall and with good posture. Use your arms to demonstrate and correct students, but otherwise stand with your arms behind your back or in front of your body holding the other hand. You shouldn't stand in one spot for the entire class, fold your arms, lean on the wall, or sit down (unless you're demonstrating something). This sounds obvious but it isn't, and all these things can make a class (and an instructor) look unprofessional.

Never use your phone in class. Get a stopwatch if you need a timer. If you're using your phone to play music, leave it in a spot away from everyone. Do not walk around with a phone in your hand.

Lesson plans

You should always have written lesson plans so that other instructors can refer to these if needed. Plan the week and month ahead in line with upcoming events like grading, tournaments and the syllabus objectives. The plan should include what the students will be doing in each class, what the warm-up will be and what equipment is needed. The second in command (2iC) should be familiar with what is happening in class and briefed by the lead instructor before starting. Memorise the lesson plan as best you can but refer back to it when needed. Don't walk around with it in your hand, this isn't professional.

You need at least one but preferably two 2iCs, especially for the younger classes. The more, the better. They can be used to take registers, hold pads and correct students. They don't need to be black belts. Older children for the small kids' classes or someone a few belts ahead for the big kids, either from their class or the adults. If you have two or three people to help, it makes life a lot easier. Over the course of time, some of your 2iCs will become even more helpful, laying the foundation for becoming instructors.

Greeting and appropriate touch

All students should be greeted by every instructor, helper, and staff member as they arrive. Smile, use their name, shake hands, and give a high five or fist bump. Use name tags for new students. Make it your job to learn everyone's name.

Touch is really important. It's how we bond and feel love and connection. But it needs to be appropriate to the situation and cannot be forced or it is awkward. When you see students, or if they do something well, give them a high five or a fist bump. Do the same with the parents, or shake hands. Post-Covid-19, the fist bump is a good choice.

Mat chat

This is a great way to interact and connect with students and should be done at appropriate times such as warm-ups, stretching, or when correcting students. Speak to them for a few moments about anything they are doing or have done already. It can be about holidays, gradings, tournaments – anything. Once you're teaching regularly, this will come naturally since you will know your students. Mat chat is great for bonding and makes students feel important.

Avoiding distractions

When running a class, it's important to make sure that you have the students' attention. Young ones get distracted easily, so it's important to set them up for success. When positioning your students, and especially if you split into multiple groups within one class, make sure the students can only see their instructor. If they are facing the other groups, the viewing area, another instructor, mirrors or windows, they will look at these instead. Consider if there are other sources of distractions, like sunlight or noises, doors that keep opening. All possible distractions should be identified and addressed to ensure maximum attention.

Mirroring

When demonstrating a move, you should always mirror. Young kids tend to mirror naturally. If you tell students to use their left stance, then you should be in your right stance when facing them. If you want them to punch with their right hand, you should demonstrate with the left. The only time you don't mirror is if you are in a big circle; the reason for this is that only half of the group is facing you, the others will be in the same or a similar position.

Praise, correct and praise

If students need correcting, be sure to first tell them what they have done well and then tell them the correction. Once they have corrected the move, praise them again and use appropriate touch. This is especially important for beginner classes. We don't do it as much with the advanced groups as we are trying to create urgency and add pressure at this stage to progress to the next level. By this stage of their training, you'll have a relationship with your students and their families, so you don't need to sugarcoat it – they know your intentions are good.

Use of voice

The level of excitement within the class is a reflection of the instructor's excitement. Start the class with a question that requires a 'Yes sir' or 'Yes ma'am' answer, making sure they repeat it if it's not loud enough. Push the students out of their comfort zone. Make sure they know that they are in class. Don't start your warm-up at maximum volume, work up to it. As the exercises get more intense, your voice and commands should get more intense with them. Work harder than the students, using your energy to motivate them. When stretching at the end of class, bring down your volume and tone. Use your voice to control the energy in classes. Have students use their voice, to shout or count. This raises class energy. Remember, enthusiasm is caught, not taught. Smile and make sure everyone says 'Thank you' when you work them extra hard.

ELITE MARTIAL ARTS INSTRUCTOR

Always be at level ten

Most people in the UK aren't particularly happy. I'd say the average person walks around at a five or six out of ten (with ten being the happiest you can be). It's probably lower in some parts of the UK. As an instructor, if you have a bad day, you can't bring this to work or you will bring the whole class down. Even if you are not feeling it, switch it off and be the best instructor you can be by delivering the best class possible. If someone comes into your class at five and they leave at a seven or eight, they will keep coming back. Be a ten, no matter what, and act, talk and walk like you're the most confident instructor in the world. Work hard every minute you're there. Every class you take should be the best class you have ever done.

Three points of contact

All instructors should have three points of contact with every student. This way you won't miss anyone and make them feel unimportant. A point of contact can be the use of a name, eye contact, a smile, appropriate touch, corrections, mat chat etc. It's easy to give more of your attention to the children who are either misbehaving or are especially good, but if you make sure you have three points of contact with every student, no one will feel left out.

Three ways of teaching

There are three different ways people can learn: audio, visual and kinaesthetic. Visual learning is learning from what you see. Sometimes, visual learners can watch something and then be able to do it without much help. The students who pick martial arts up easily tend to learn this way. Audio learners need things to be described in more detail and might not pick things up from the visual demonstration alone. Most instructors cover both visual and audio learning, but kinaesthetic learning tends to get overlooked.

You tend to find that very young children and children with learning difficulties are more kinaesthetic learners, meaning they learn by touch. For example, you might be telling a student to punch using their right hand. You are showing them with your right hand and pointing to their right hand and saying 'right hand', but they just aren't getting it. With these students, you need to grab their right hand and punch with it so that they feel how they need to move. You'll notice this even more when teaching grappling, as you sometimes need to physically put students in the correct position so that they can feel it. Explaining and demos alone are often not enough. Some students must feel in order to learn.

Focus claps

These are pattern breakers and are used throughout kids' classes. When the children start to get over-excited and their focus shifts to what's going on outside, they go into visual mode. Even if you shout their name, they may not hear you. They aren't being rude; they are just hyper-focused on their current point of interest. A focus clap pulls the students out of visual mode and into audio mode. This breaks their pattern and allows them to listen.

There are many ways to use pattern breakers. You can shout 'Focus clap one' and then clap once, 'Focus clap two' and clap twice, 'Focus clap three' and clap three times. Train the children to stop what they're doing immediately when they hear these shouts and start clapping along with the instructor. This pulls them back into the class, so they stop and watch the instructor. On the last focus clap, make sure to spring to attention and stand still, and tell them to do the same. Look around the room for a child that is not moving at all. If they aren't still enough, do it all again. Once you identify who was the fastest and the stillest, point them out and give them a high five or fist bump. You can change the attention position to a sitting position if you are in a grappling class and on the floor.

The more you use these focus claps and pattern breakers, the more control you will have. You can also use them as a way to move to the next part of the lesson or class.

Countdowns

Countdowns are a great way to create urgency. Count down from five to one when you ask the students to switch partners, go and get equipment or get themselves back in line. Anyone who is late gets press-ups and the fastest gets rewarded. Countdowns keep the energy up and are fun.

Competing

Children are naturally competitive. Use this to make classes more fun, keep the children engaged and create and maintain high energy. If you demand that a child stands still, they won't. But if you get the children to compete against each other to see who can stand the stillest, all of a sudden it's a game they want to win. Do this with exercises and races. Encourage the competitive instinct and nurture it. They will need this later in their training for tournaments, as well as in life.

Syllabus and grading

Your syllabus is your best retention tool. It should ideally have eight to twelve belts as a minimum. When I re-designed my syllabus, I put extra stripe belts in and simplified the start of the journey, adding more fitness. This allowed new students to enjoy their training, get fitter and work on the basics that are needed at the earlier stages.

The belt system shouldn't be overly complicated. You want a slow start syllabus that gets more challenging. When structured like this, it allows for better student retention and more freedom to create exciting and varied lesson plans and not have to stick to strict syllabus guidelines. A complicated syllabus doesn't make a good fighter. I know world champions who only use three techniques. This doesn't mean not teaching students everything you know, but not everything needs to be in the syllabus.

Set up milestone events at key grades, like fitness, running, sparring, grappling tests and tournaments. Make sure that all students fight or compete in some type of competition and buy the kit at key points to support the new element of their training.

The black belt should be the hardest thing they have ever attempted. Everything in the syllabus should build up to it. It's better if the black belt test is taken by a third party or other instructors. To see an example of our black belt, there is a video on YouTube. Search 'British military martial arts black belt grading' documentary or go to www.leematthewsofficial.com to watch it.

At my schools, regular gradings are done every three months and split into two tags. These are done monthly, with the third month for grading. The syllabus material for each grade is split in half, with the first two completed in class. The third month is official grading in a formal setting where students go for their belt. This means that if the students train regularly, every month they can be assessed. This keeps students interested and engaged so that they improve and stay longer. Log attendance and only allow students to be graded if they have attended the required number of classes. This holds them accountable.

Competition

When you look at a winner or champion, you see the end product. If they are winning at the top level, it would be reasonable to believe that they must be somehow unlike everyone else, or built differently to their competition. This couldn't be further from the truth.

I remember playing football in the playground as a kid; some of the boys were much better than everyone else, myself included. Growing up, I was under the assumption that people were either good at football or they weren't. I think most people who don't compete in sports have this assumption. The reality was that the boys in my school playground had played a substantial amount more than me. They played before school, during the first morning break, at lunchtime, in the second break and after school. They played in the fields when they got home. Most of the good ones played for at least one team and would attend training and matches. Jumping in at random lunch times and thinking that you would be anywhere near their standard was just madness. By age eleven, these lads had been doing this for two to three years. They had played thousands of hours already. Imagine how good you would be if you spent thousands of hours enthusiastically doing anything. Even if you started out bad, you would eventually get pretty good. This is the case for anything, from sports to business, that involves a degree of skill.

The dyslexic child who can't read or write well and so avoids any opportunity to do either will get worse and their confidence will decrease, to the point that they are hugely disadvantaged as an adult. But even a twenty-five-year-old who can barely read or write could learn if they had a strong enough reason to do so, perhaps like starting their own business. They will spend thousands of hours over many years practising because they have no choice, and they will start to improve. I know this to be true because this was me. That twenty-five-year-old is today writing a book. It just takes practice and a good enough reason.

If you look back in time at the champion on the podium, they weren't always on top. No matter how good they are now, they were once a beginner. No one starts off winning everything. Losing is one of the best self-development tools there is. As long as you stay on task and are around the right people, doing the correct practice, eventually you will start to win. As a competitive martial artist, or in any other competitive sport, you learn this lesson early. It's the losses and the lessons you learn from them that humble you, strengthen your character, build your resilience, teach you the best lessons and set the foundation for your future growth.

Keep failing your way to the top. Fight the good ones over and over again and lose, until one day you don't lose as badly and you take that lesson with you. At this point, you chase them and train harder – you know you're close. The next time you fight and are neck and neck, you know that winning is inevitable – eventually, it is going to happen. Even if it's not that fight, you will win at some stage as long as you keep showing up. This is the process – there are no shortcuts. It's been tested over time and is simple, but not easy. Indeed, it's hard to walk that path. It takes tremendous character development to live this life.

Sparring/grappling or some type of combat with your students in a competitive environment is vital if you are genuinely interested in developing them to the best of their abilities. If you're not great at this side of things, find others who can help you.

We have a few fight teams within BMMA that fight in the open tournaments and are extremely successful. Tony Anderton, who coaches one of the teams, joined BMMA aged twenty. He left his job as a manager at McDonald's and went on our five-day training course over ten years ago and has been with us ever since. He now has two full-time martial arts centres, in Rugeley and Kidsgrove and has built up his fight team, Team SAS. His team won the most medals out of all of the other clubs in the UK at the WAKO British Championships in 2023. His approach to coaching mirrors the principles and ideas in this book and he travels all over the world with his team, who have won multiple British, European and world titles.

Team SAS – the number one ranked team in the UK, 19 February 2023. Left to right: Peter Edwards, Ethan Kerr, Darrell Merryweather, Ellie Harvey, Tony Anderton, Jack Buckley, Summer Harvey, Lola Lloyd and Neville Wray

We also have a female instructor, Charlotte Craighill, who has been with BMMA for over twelve years and is now an area commander with two full-time centres and multiple satellite schools in Leeds. She runs a fighting squad and one of her students, Dantrell Mitchell-Knight, has just been selected for the national TKD squad where he will train as a full-time professional fighter.

Competition is vital to the growth of your students and the integrity of your school.

Dantrell Mitchell-Knight and Charlotte Craighill sporting their Team England WKKC tops

Income stream generators

Income stream generators are a great way of not only bringing in extra revenue, but also creating value and useful services for your students. This helps with retention and community building. Below I will briefly introduce some easy to implement income stream generators you can use in your business.

Upgrades

Students often move up to another class or start extra classes. They will usually need a new suit or equipment for this, which is explained in advance for the benefit of the parents. The children and students are normally excited to move up and the equipment will benefit their progression.

Kit sales

The normal sparring kits and suits that are needed at each new level are integrated into the syllabus, with add-ons like bags, tracksuits, hats, hoodies and T-shirts. You can sell these from your pro shop if you have a full-time venue. If not, create an online shop. Find a local printer that can fulfil your orders. Make sure all items have your logo on them and the students will be walking billboards flying the flag of your school everywhere they go.

Seminars

Extra learning activities are a great way to raise student standards, keep them coming regularly and bring in extra income.

Karate parties

These are great fun and only take place on the weekends. They will also provide you with a load of prospects, so make sure to get people's details so they can be contacted at a later date with a great offer. We normally charge a minimum of £10 per head with a max of twenty children. Parents bring the food, you supply the games and fun.

Boot camps

Offering one-off courses with a set fee and start date works really well for adults. The main ones are beginner adults, ladies-only, or military-style boot camps (non-martial arts). They run for around six weeks. In the end, a good amount of the attendees will sign up as regular students as they will have bought into the community and would definitely have got fitter and lost weight if you have been running the classes correctly and holding them accountable.

Social events

It's great if you can get all of your students and their parents together at least once a month. Christmas parties, awards ceremonies, interclub tournaments, trips to theme parks, BBQs, paintballing, adventure training weekends and running clubs are all great. Make sure you charge when you organise these as they take time to organise and create a lot of value.

Fight nights

These are a great way to introduce your students to competitive environments as they are within your control and involve only your students. Match all fighters as closely as possible and control the amount of contact so that it's safe. Only allow each student one fight so that they can get used to the nerves, and give a trophy or medal for first and second place. Have selection training days to choose who will be fighting. You should charge the fighters for entry and spectators for watching the fight, with a fee for the selection training session.

Interclub tournaments

Interclub competitions are always going on at our full-time training centres. If you don't have a centre, partner up with someone who does or rent a hall somewhere. Tournaments are another good way of introducing your students to competition in a controlled environment before sending them out into the big bad tournament world. You can link these in with seminars where you go over the rules, have or show demo fights and make it an educational and enjoyable day for students.

Mentoring

Mentoring is such an important part of learning and improving. You don't need to reinvent the wheel, just look for who is good at what you want to be good at and spend some time with them. For me, I didn't have just one mentor who had everything I wanted. I had lots of people who I admired in many different areas of life and I unconsciously modelled what I liked about them and wanted to improve in myself.

When I served in the military, I had so many positive male role models. Even if I wasn't fully aware of it at the time, being around so many men, my own age and older, who thought highly of themselves and classed themselves as a cut above everyone else, had a big impact on me. When my journey moved into martial arts and the fighting world, I met a lot of new people and, because of my background, I gravitated to the guys at the top. I loved to feel the gap between where they were and where I was and try and bridge it. I would go as far as to say that you can't reach a high level of success in anything unless you can feel that gap and know the right people to teach you how to bridge it. Mentors don't need to walk around with you, finding life lessons in every experience, like Mr Miyagi. You just need to be around people who are better than you at something and it will rub off.

I was extremely lucky to be mentored by John Jepson and Leigh Childs, who at the time were the most successful school owners in the UK and pioneers in the industry. They probably didn't even realise that I followed everything they said to the letter. I was also lucky enough to have many mentors and friends in the martial arts fighting world. One, in particular, was Drew Neal. He was to become one of the best points fighters from the UK of his era, in my opinion, but we didn't yet realise that at the time. To me, he was a good friend and a brilliant fighter. Over the course of ten years, we did everything together. We travelled around the world fighting together with the WAKO GB team and as part of our TopTen UK team. Looking back now, we competed ferociously against each other in training and in life, and pushed each other to new heights. We held each other accountable. We were always comparing our training and diets. Sparring sessions would often get intense but would always calm down and we'd laugh about it at the end. When facing anyone else in the world, we were the best of friends.

RETENTION (THE BATTLE)

Lee and Drew Neal on the cover of Martial Arts Illustrated, *November 2011*

ELITE MARTIAL ARTS INSTRUCTOR

Lee and Drew Neal at a photoshoot in Germany

Lee and Drew at the TopTen British Open Championships at Bodypower

Lee with Lee Sansum

I was also lucky enough to meet a good friend, Lee Sansum (author of *The Bodyguard*).[9] He was fifteen years older than me, also ex-military, and always had time for me. His martial arts skills, teaching ability and understanding of business were some of the best I've seen in the industry. I even stayed at Lee's house in the Scottish Highlands to train for my WAKO Pro European title fight in Derry,

---

9   L Sansum, *The Bodyguard* (Seven Dials, 2022)

Northern Ireland in 2006. I was with Lee for a full week before the fight, training three times a day in a real-life karate kid scenario. We had a game plan, which we stuck to. On the night, everything went exactly to plan and I won convincingly. Lee's son, Damon, came along to watch and support me and we became close too. Damon grew into a world-class fighter himself and moved from kickboxing to the GB Olympic TKD team, where he fought full-time for over ten years.

Lee and Damon Sansum wild camping in the Lake District at the annual adventure training retreat

Summary

This round has focused on retention. The military analogy of the battle, as any school owner will tell you, is appropriate when it comes to keeping hold of your students. It's so important to have the right structures in place to service your students correctly or they will soon dwindle in number. We've learned about the importance of monitoring the key stats for your school, so you know where you are and where you need to go. We've gone over the best practice for managing your dojo, including how to organise your classes, the syllabus and gradings, how to conduct yourself as an instructor and the importance of mentors.

In Round 5 we will go over the restructuring of your school and how to set it up for continued success and growth.

PART THREE
MAKE A DIFFERENCE

Now you have launched and grown your school, you need to structure it in such a way that you are planting seeds for the future while rearranging things so that it's not you doing all of the work. You want to create a legacy, something that can positively impact as many lives as possible and support you and your family in the long term, both financially and spiritually.

ROUND 5
Restructure (Reorg)

In this round, we will be covering the restructure of your school and business. The military analogy for this stage is the 'Reorg', which takes place after an attack. Once you have fought through the enemy position, you stop to re-evaluate the situation and move forwards in a positive direction.

On 27 February 1942, men from C Company, 2 Para commanded by Major JD Frost raided a radar station at Bruneval in France. The mission was a success: they achieved their objective, seizing not only the radar they had been tasked to capture, but also two German radar technicians.

On the night of 11–12 June 1982 in the Falkland Islands, Sergeant Ian McKay VC was the platoon Sergeant of four platoons, B Company. 3 Para had been tasked (along with the rest of the battalion) with taking Mount Longdon in one of the bloodiest battles of the war. His platoon came under heavy fire from a machine gun position. He, along with three other men, broke cover and charged the position. All other members of this small group were killed or injured, so he continued by himself, took out the position and was sadly killed in the last moments of victory. His selfless act helped give 3 Para the momentum to win the battle. Sergeant McKay was posthumously awarded the Victoria Cross for his bravery.

When on Operation Herrick in Afghanistan on 20 August 2006, Corporal Brian Budd VC from A Company, 3 Para, was part of a patrol that took incoming fire while in an exposed cornfield. To save the lives of his men he rushed to the position with a full-frontal

RESTRUCTURE (REORG)

attack, killing three Taliban and himself in the process. His actions allowed his section to pull back to safety. Brain Budd was then posthumously awarded the Victoria Cross for bravery.

What these great men did helped shape how I do business today, by following the same principles they and their platoons would have followed. Even once the attack has been won and the last position has been cleared, the job still isn't finished.

The British Army has been doing this for years under many different names, systems and mnemonics, but it has always been based on the same principles. The same is true in martial arts: winning a round doesn't win the fight. When you have won the battle, you still haven't won the war. You must regroup, reflect and get ready to do it all again. This is known as the regroup of the platoon or a reorganisation of the section ('Regroup/Reorg').

The first step is to ensure the safety of your section/platoon. All troops are issued with arcs of fire that must be covered to ensure the groups' protection. These arcs will be 260 degrees and each soldier will cover an area that overlaps with the soldier next to them to maintain complete effective protection.

Next, you check ammunition so that the section and platoon commanders know what is left and can re-distribute accordingly until a resupply is available. Casualties are then centralised to be dealt with appropriately and sections are reorganised to account for the new numbers. The equipment is checked to see what's been lost and allocated soldiers will start searching enemy casualties for any intelligence that could help with the mission.

The platoon will then either dig in to protect themselves from enemy bombardment or deploy with urgency to leave the area to protect casualties from enemy follow-ups if necessary. The next round of orders will then be distributed, and the mission continues from there.

This reflects the processes you'll go through in Round 5, which is the restructure ('Reorg') of your school. Once you have achieved your objective from the earlier rounds, you need to look at the business structure: where you are, what's changed and what adjustments need to happen to move forward and grow.

Military structures

Effective military structures have been tried and tested over hundreds of years and the British model is copied throughout the world. By understanding these structures and roles, you can see how they can be used to help train students, mentor instructors and control the command structure in your business for maximum efficiency.

RESTRUCTURE (REORG)

- **Buddy, Buddy system:** This is the first thing that you will learn about in the army, regardless of the regiment. You are always with someone. You won't even go to the toilet without your buddy. You cook together and you sleep in the same area. When one of you takes your weapon apart to clean it, the other one covers you. This is a great system for many reasons, but mainly accountability and backup. In business and in life, make sure your buddy has the same goals and objectives as you.

- **Fire teams:** Each soldier is placed in a fire team of four to six people. These are the people who you work and do everything else with. You will be in the same room in camp and right next to each other in the field.

- **Sections:** A section consists of eight to twelve people, made up of two fire teams, Charlie and Delta. Delta will have one member in charge (Lance Corporal) who is the 2iC. The section commander (Corporal) will be in charge of Charlie and the overall command of the section. If the section commander is not around, then the 2iC will take over. Even if you don't get along with everyone in your section, you must work together professionally.

- **Platoons:** A platoon consists of three sections and an HQ element comprising a Platoon Commander, a Lieutenant and a Platoon Sergeant. There will also be a runner and radio operator responsible for communication. Platoons are normally around thirty to forty people in size.

- **Companies:** A company consists of three to four platoons and an HQ element. In total, it's no more than 120–150 people. The army knows that this is the optimal size for maximum cohesion. Everything you do in the army is with your company. No matter how big the battle group is, you only work within your company. The HQ element has a Major in charge and a Sergeant Major 2iC, with the Colour Sergeant as Quartermaster in charge of supplies. There are also admin staff and junior NCOs within the company HQ.

- **Battalions:** These are regiment subunits and consist of 450–600 soldiers, which is generally four to five companies and an HQ element. A Lieutenant Colonel is in charge overall and the Regiment Sergeant Major is in charge of the discipline. Together, they command all the companies.

- **Regiments:** A regiment consists of two to four battalions. In the case of the Parachute Regiment, this has three regular battalions and one reserve with at least 1,800 soldiers. These numbers are approximate and will vary slightly for different types of units and their purpose.

The army is fully aware that having different regiments encourages competition. The regiments compete fiercely against each other in everything they do, but they join together to create one of the best armies in the world when facing a common enemy during a real war. This is how we need to see ourselves as martial arts instructors and coaches. We should compete against each other to bring up the standards but join together when needed.

All of these group sizes are in line with British anthropologist Robert Dunbar's model of group sizes for maximum cohesion.[10] Dunbar believes that an individual can only maintain a stable relationship with around 150 people. Any bigger and you don't get close and can't remember everyone's names.

He goes on to say that the tightest circle is around five people (fire team). That's followed by fifteen to twenty good friends (platoon), 150 meaningful contacts (company), 500 acquaintances (battalion), and 1,500 people who you'd recognise (regiment).

These group sizes are something you must think about as you grow and develop your business. Where possible, we have used this theory to structure classes, schools, a collection of schools and instructors. We also use it when training and

---

10 RIM Dunbar, 'Coevolution of neocortical size, group size and language in humans', *Behavioral and Brain Sciences*, 16/4 (1993), 681–694, https://doi.org/10.1017/S0140525X00032325

mentoring instructors, with buddies and fire teams for small groups, for accountability and to ensure maximum effectiveness.

Exceeding these group sizes changes the group dynamics and they will either need reducing in size, splitting down into multiple smaller groups, or additional help and support.

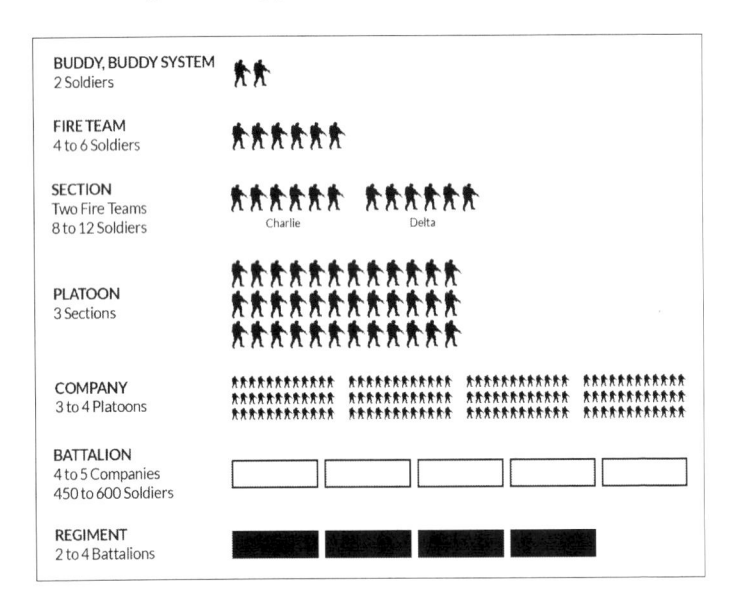

BUDDY, BUDDY SYSTEM 2 Soldiers	
FIRE TEAM 4 to 6 Soldiers	
SECTION Two Fire Teams 8 to 12 Soldiers	Charlie Delta
PLATOON 3 Sections	
COMPANY 3 to 4 Platoons	
BATTALION 4 to 5 Companies 450 to 600 Soldiers	
REGIMENT 2 to 4 Battalions	

Improvise, adapt and overcome

Joining the military totally changed me and the direction of my life. I was a different man after training. I took risks and thought outside the box. I became resourceful and found ways to get the job done. I was

RESTRUCTURE (REORG)

trained to be self-sufficient but also work with others when needed.

In the army, we re-shaped reality around our objective and made it happen. We were taught to think on our feet and, if we didn't know the answer or the solution, to figure it out. This produced men with immense confidence and competence in extreme situations.

Knowing that you can and will find a solution means you start to become more comfortable in situations that are out of your control. This doesn't stop at your job; it extends to your general life. I've heard stories of ex-paratroopers landing amazing jobs by stretching the truth a little and then nailing the job they totally bluffed their way into. Sometimes, you have to bet the ranch and take big risks if there are possible big returns, but only when you are starting out. You put all of your eggs in one basket, but you watch that basket closely and make sure you achieve the objective. I've also seen people get out of serious situations by bluffing, and acting like they're calm and confident even when they're not.

For example, there was an incident in Newcastle when a big fight broke out between one of the platoons and a large door team from a few of the bars on the street. During the chaos, a few well-placed roundhouse kicks were thrown at the doormen by one of the members of the platoon before escaping. One of the guys somehow ended up inside the club and found himself surrounded by the door team who had picked themselves up off the floor by then. They cornered him and he had to think on his feet, so he jumped into an over-exaggerated kung fu fighting stance, with a few noises for extra effect. The door team immediately jumped back assuming he was also a highly trained martial artist, after what they had just witnessed outside. This allowed him a moment to escape.

Another example is when we went on a recruiting drive for our TopTen UK team. We had an extremely strong team already but there were some other amazing UK fighters we wanted to recruit to take the team to the next level. We needed a big reason for them to join. If it was just them going for the team, that might not have been enough, so we contacted a handful of the best fighters in the UK; together with the existing members, we knew they'd make a world-class team. I may have also stretched the truth a little, telling all the potential new team members that the other top fighters we were trying to recruit were pretty much in the team already, as long as they joined too, and that if they all joined, the team would be unstoppable. They all rang each other to confirm this, and all joined together. Separately, they might not have had enough reason to join, so we had to create a bigger vision that everyone could buy into. They went on to become one of the best teams in the world.

I started my martial arts school with no money at all of my own. I was entitled to some resettlement money from the army when I left if I could find a career transition course but there were no martial arts courses back then, so my instructor at the time and myself quickly put one together. I could then use my portion of the money, plus a loan from the bank, to open my first martial arts centre. I managed to negotiate three months' rent for free as the place was run down and I committed to a longer lease. By the time that three months had elapsed, I had enough students to pay the rent, the loan and more than enough to cover my house, bills, and spending, while also getting a brand-new sports car. I had to get off the ground somehow, so I took a few calculated risks.

These are just a few examples of being resourceful and finding a way to get what you want, or to get out of something you don't want. This is a helpful skill to have if you want to be successful.

Like Arnold Schwarzenegger said, 'Break the rules, not the law, but break the rules. It's impossible to be a maverick or a true original if you're too well behaved and don't want to break the rules.'

Find a way to make it happen. Ask for forgiveness, not permission.

Growth structure

Let's look at how to grow your school to the point where you have a big team with multiple locations.

First, you need to make sure your school is set up correctly with the right classes available. When you first start out, you should be using the basic model of Little Soldiers, Cadets and adult classes. This is great for the launch stage, but once you reach the rapid growth phase, you'll need to adjust to allow for new students.

Make sure that at least half of your classes are for beginners. At first, everyone is a beginner, but they will progress; if you want to expand, you need to make sure that there is always a beginners' class. The types of martial arts schools that struggle are those that are top-heavy, with more advanced students than beginners.

In order to be successful, it needs to be the other way around. Your school needs to be bottom-heavy, with lots of beginners. These are your most loyal students – the new students are the ones who are keen on bringing in referrals and buying all the kit etc. But also bear in mind that any changes you make in your school will be met with resistance from the people who have been there longer. While you still need to meet the needs of the long-standing students, you can't make decisions based solely on what makes them happy, as they will all want the school to stay exactly as it is.

THE STRUCTURE OF A MARTIAL ARTS SCHOOL

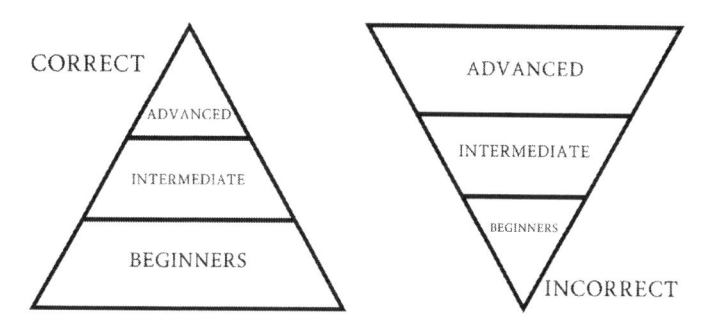

CORRECT — triangle (top to bottom): ADVANCED / INTERMEDIATE / BEGINNERS

INCORRECT — inverted triangle (top to bottom): ADVANCED / INTERMEDIATE / BEGINNERS

The ideal school should look like the structure on the left.

You are at the top, as the main instructor, with the other senior grades below. Then come the intermediate students, with loads of beginners at the bottom. This is how a successful school will look.

A school that's not set up for growth will look more like the structure on the right.

Here, the school and classes are based around the higher-grade students or fighters. Not many new members will come to this school and, if they do, they won't stay long because the classes aren't suited to their ability. Fighters don't want to pay for classes, they already have the kit and they either aren't as interested in grading or they are already senior grades. A lot of successful fight teams only have thirty to fifty members in their school, but everyone is top level. All of the classes are catered to them, and new members are few and far between.

If you have 300 students in your school, because it is properly structured for success, you will have a bigger pool of students to pick from if you want to create a fight team. The best of these can compete for a spot. Have them and their parents sign a contract agreeing to the terms of the training and fighting and they are yours to train as you please. You will get a better-quality fighter this way, as they have to earn the spot and aren't allowed to fight in competition until they do. These should be separate classes away from the main students, though if you let the fighters mix with the regular students in the advanced and sparring classes then over time, the standard of the entire school will rise.

Building a team of staff

When you start out, you're normally doing everything by yourself. Most instructors believe only they can do things the way they need to be done. As soon as they try to pull back, even for a random night off, they will get phone calls and complaints from parents and students. Sound familiar?

I ran every one of my classes six days a week, with six classes a day, training in the advanced classes and training in the morning. I then fought at tournaments on weekends. I lived like that for the first ten years that I taught. I felt stuck and like I couldn't step back because if I did, everyone would leave.

You need staff to ease the pressure. First, an administrator will relieve you of over half the workload. They can book intros, track statistics, sell and order the equipment, promote events and communicate with students and parents. Sometimes, even a parent is able to help with this. A dedicated admin is ideal, as that is all they need to do – they won't need to worry about teaching.

Next, you need to get as many 2iCs (seconds-in-command) as you can. They are the building blocks for future instructors. Pick from the adults or ladies-only classes, or use Cadets with a few belts for the Little Soldiers' classes. You should constantly be recruiting from your students.

The biggest step for some schools is letting another instructor start taking some of the classes. Try and get one from within the ranks of your school, if possible. They don't need to be as good as you, but they should be friendly, charismatic and energetic. At first, have them take beginner classes. This eliminates half of your teaching obligations. You can then adjust your schedule to make sure that you get a day or two off in the week and will be more available in the evening to work and speak with students and parents. Use this time to focus on the business and mentor the instructor. You will soon replace anyone who leaves or doesn't support your changes. You will still be serving your advanced and intermediate students and fight teams, so there will be minimum disruption for these students.

If you want to pull back further, the next step is to get all of the Little Soldiers' classes covered, as well as all beginners and intermediate classes. If you take this step, after about a year of handing over the beginners' classes, there will be less resistance. You can then run only the advanced classes, sparring/grappling classes and the intros and fighter classes. This only takes a few days of your time, giving you more space to focus on growing the school.

No matter how good the new instructor is, people will complain if their classes change. Some will leave when you step back or replace a current instructor, as they get used to a certain person's style. Stick to your guns and understand that this is normal. Make decisions for the school based on what works for you, your life and your family. After a few weeks, it will be the new normal. New students enrolling won't know any different. Be strong and weather the storm when students and parents react. Remember, if you're uncomfortable and getting pushback, it's a sign that you're changing – change is good.

Once the school has been running for a few years, you will start getting more competent advanced students and black belts. Train them up via the instructor training programme and selection method that is presented in the next round, then you can start thinking about opening up more locations.

In general, your core team of staff should be made up of the following job roles:

- The **Special Winning Attitude Team (SWAT)** or **Super Attitude Students (SAS):** These are members of your school or their parents who help a main instructor in classes.

- **Assistant instructor:** Someone who has completed the instructor training course and is in their probation period. They assist the main instructors in class, take warm-ups and parts of classes under guidance but also provide cover when instructors are off.

- **Instructor:** Someone who can run classes and has passed the training course and probation period.

- **Lead instructor:** Runs classes and is able to be independent from your HQ. Either employed or self-employed as a franchisee.

- **Area commanders:** Has a team of instructors working under them. Like lead instructors, they can be either employed or self-employed as a franchisee.

- **HQ:** This is the command element of the business, where your central team is based.

Extended team

Your 'team' doesn't just comprise your instructors and core staff members, it includes anyone who is involved with your business. It's important to remember that everyone, including your extended team, must create value and help move you in the right direction. Anyone who is not in line with the school values must go.

Your extended team members include the following.

- **Accountants:** Make sure that they are good and know the industry – a good accountant can save you a tremendous amount of money if they are doing their job properly and understand your business.

- **Billing companies:** These are the companies that take tuition payments. They can be a valuable part of your team and help with many aspects of the business. They can also help you network with other like-minded instructors.

- **Solicitors:** The bigger you get, the more necessary these are. It's important to have legal protection in everything that you do. For example, when signing a lease on a new centre, without the correct advice you can end up personally liable, which puts your family's future at risk. If you're employing instructors or have franchisees, you need the proper agreements in place. Don't take the easy way out; use a professional and take care of it properly.

- **Franchisors:** A franchise is a great way to get ahead and also access valuable guidance and networks. Following a blueprint that has been proven to work makes it easier to succeed. Like anything, there are good and bad franchisors so find one that's in line with your values and outlook that adds value, so you can grow together.

Business structures[11]

One of the first decisions you will make when starting your business is what structure, or legal entity, to use. It's important to consider factors such as what your business will do, if it will have employees, whether you will be working with others or by yourself and, of course, expected turnover levels, as these will dictate which is the right way forward.

There are several ways to structure your business, each with its own benefits and drawbacks and different taxation rules and regulations to follow. While it's not uncommon for a business to change structures as it

---

[11] All information provided by Maple Accountancy

grows and evolves, it certainly helps to get a good footing to begin with so that you can focus on the growth of the business. Below, I'll run through the different ways you can structure your martial arts business.

Sole trader

One of the most common ways to set up a business, and often how people start out as self-employed, is as a sole trader. This is essentially a business owned and operated by one individual, with the business considered an extension of the individual, rather than a separate legal entity. As such, it is one of the simplest setups as there are fewer filing requirements and obligations. However, this lack of separation between the individual and the business comes with greater risk, as any debts or liabilities will be linked to the individual and not just the business. As a sole trader, the individual must also pay income tax on all profits made by the business, which would also be combined with any other sources of personal income they have (such as rental income, PAYE earnings or a pension), with less opportunity to manage taxes efficiently.

Partnership

A partnership is similar to the sole trader setup with comparable requirements, but has two or more individuals running the business. In this arrangement, each individual will have ownership of and responsibility for the business as well as the profits; by default, ownership is viewed as equal, but exact details can be modified through a partnership agreement.

Limited company (LTD)

Limited companies are often the best solution for businesses, as they can come in all different shapes and sizes and offer the most flexibility. A limited company is a separate legal entity, which provides a certain amount of protection for the owners and offers various tax advantages. The limited company will be required to complete an annual set of accounts and tax returns in order to calculate the corporation tax it owes on its profits. This is separate from the owner's tax liability, and they would still be required to pay tax on drawings from the company either through salary or dividends, which would be declared on a personal tax return. The dividends are taxed at lower rates as they are based on the profits of the company, so while there are more responsibilities and filing requirements with this setup, they do offer more potential for tax savings.

Limited liability partnership (LLP)

An LLP is a cross between a limited company and a partnership and is commonly used by professional practices, such as law firms, though any type of business can operate as an LLP, and they can be suitable for use in a joint venture as an alternative to a limited company. An LLP must have at least two designated members and is required to make filings at Companies House to show the financial situation and acting members, similar to what is required of a limited company. However, unlike the limited company, the LLP itself is not taxed; instead, it is the members who are taxed on their share of the profits, just as partners would be in a partnership. This means that, while they operate as a separate entity from the owners, they do not offer the same tax flexibility.

Multicompany structure

It is possible to have multiple limited companies and there is no real restriction on the number of limited companies you can be a director of. Having multiple companies may be beneficial in terms of keeping different business interests or elements separate from each other, allowing you to clearly see how each is performing, as well as mitigating the risk of a failing part of your overall business interests impacting the successful ones.

It is also possible to use a holding company to allow you to consolidate your ownership of multiple companies into one entity, making it easier to manage your tax affairs. There are, however, strict HMRC rules on what is allowed to be grouped within a holding company – there must be a legitimate business reason for doing so, not just a tax reason, otherwise this could be deemed as artificial separation.

International companies

Setting up an offshore or international company can be complicated, as you will need to consider not only the tax and governance legislation of the country you are incorporated in but also the ones you operate in or supply to, as well as the tax relationships between them. Any reason to be set up offshore needs to be strictly business-related and well thought through. I would recommend you speak to a professional adviser if you are considering this option.

Deciding which business structure is best suited to your school will depend upon a host of factors, including your longer-term plans for the business, whether or not you need the protection of limited liability, the legal and administrative obligations you are willing to take on and also whether you are looking for inward investment.

If you are contemplating a new business venture, it's best to speak to a professional adviser in the first instance so that they can help you choose the best structure for your particular circumstances and avoid any costly mistakes.

Negotiating

Everything in life is a negotiation. There are a few different possible outcomes of most negotiations. If you are buying an item like a car or house from someone, you want the best price. Understandably, both parties are trying to get the best out of the deal. This is called a win-lose negotiation, as one of you does better than the other, but ultimately you come to an agreement.

There are also negotiations that happen in relationships, whether that's with your partner in life, work, or a friend. For example, you could be trying to secure a pay rise from the boss, or want to ask your wife if you can go to Ibiza with friends. You can't just screw someone over in this situation because you want to maintain the relationship after the negotiation. You may even need to renegotiate at a later date, or raise other issues, so you don't want to leave a bitter taste in their mouth.

In these negotiations, you need to find a win-win outcome. This is when you get what you want while also keeping the other party on your side by giving them something they want too. Being able to negotiate these kinds of outcomes is fundamental to success in your relationships and in business. Most of the time, people think of black-or-white solutions and end up not getting what they want, or getting what they want but upsetting the other party. Be creative and think outside of the box. Most of the time, there is an answer or solution that is better for both parties, but people get stuck thrashing things out. You can see their egos kicking in; they want to win and so they get emotional, almost like children. You have no chance of creative thinking when you're in this state and no chance of finding a win-win solution.

You should try to present the solution at the same time as the problem. If you keep going to your partner, your boss or business partner with problems, they are going to start associating you with negativity – no one likes or wants extra problems in their life.

You will sometimes find when negotiating with someone that they don't have the same win-win goal as you. If you've found this to be the case when you have gone to them with solutions on multiple different occasions, I personally wouldn't continue working with them. Don't burn bridges, though; it's important to stay respectful and understand that people work differently, even when you have to walk away. Challenges will constantly come up in work, business and life; we all need to understand this and try to help each other. If someone is only after a win in any negotiation, with no concern for you, then you know what you need to do.

When communicating with people about things that are important to you both, sometimes it gets emotional. It is impossible to resolve a situation if one or both parties are emotional. I am, by nature, a hot head.

When I was a younger man, I had anger issues, but now in business I am totally different. I know that if I lose my temper or get emotional, I lose. In any situation, personal or professional, never try and intimidate people to get your own way. It won't work and you will lose their respect. Be calm in the eye of the storm.

Never respond when you're angry. This is a good rule for anyone. I have had many a heated text message or someone moaning about something at 10.30pm or over a weekend, but I always wait to respond. Let's clear something up: if you are sending a heated message to someone while you are in an emotional state, then you are the problem. Sending a message with what you believe to be a major problem at a time when that person can't deal with it, or shouldn't have to, isn't a professional way to conduct yourself. If I were working with someone who did this, I would address this with them as soon as possible (but not at 10.30pm while I was still angry).

Effective communication has a lot to do with timing, especially in heated situations. Wait before responding. Don't send your response straight away. If you can, wait a full day. You can let them know that you've received their message and that you'll get back to them shortly, but don't send anything more substantive while you're angry. It's a good idea to write out your message first and have someone else read it. Change it if you feel uncomfortable about what you've written and eliminate parts that might trigger them even more. You need to keep the person calm in order to resolve the situation, not escalate it, or 'win' at their expense. Wait until the next day and remove anything that could be aggravating, word it differently or soften the tone while still communicating the same message. It's also best to respond to someone using the same form of communication that they used to contact you. If they texted you, text them back.

Address only the issues at hand, not your emotions or their emotions, which may be evident or mentioned in their message. Be polite in your response and, depending on how upset they are and what it's about, try and speak about something else first to play down the other issue(s). This suggests you are not as upset as you actually are. Remember, the goal of the message is to resolve the issue, find a win-win scenario and move forward in a positive way.

If you want to be successful and elite, then you must be able to keep people on your side while leading and growing a good team. If that means you need to go to bed thinking about something someone said that's upset you, and you end up thinking about it all night, then so be it. You need to be strong enough to wait until you are calm and can respond without emotion.

The bigger your business gets, the more situations like this will happen. It's about turning negatives into positives and finding win-win solutions. Over time, this will make you successful.

Building a community

When people join a martial arts school, they might initially join for fitness, self-defence, or weight loss reasons, but it's the community that will keep them there. It doesn't matter what style of martial arts you do 90% of the time, as most people don't know the differences and you can be successful with any style. What's important is that as you build your school, you build a positive community. If you don't, a community will build itself anyway, but without you at the head – you might find that a clique emerges, which can cause division. It needs strong leadership and great teamwork to build and maintain martial arts communities. When building a community, focus on what the individuals want out of it and try to make sure that you are supporting your students and family by providing the same things that you would want yourself in a happy and thriving environment.

The concept of the six human needs was first birthed by Sigmond Freud and more recently introduced to the general public by Anthony Robbins[12]. These six needs are fundamental to our happiness and place in the world. I first learned about them in my early twenties and have made a conscious effort to bring them to light for other people. I have always followed these

---

12 A Robbins, 'Discover the Six Human Needs', www.tonyrobbins.com/mind-meaning/do-you-need-to-feel-significant/, accessed 17 August 2023

without knowing it, but if at any time in my life I feel a bit wobbly, I look to these to see if anything is missing.

If you can fulfil all these needs, you will find yourself happier as you will be aligned with your cause. It's not easy and you have to dance a fine line between chaos and order trying to balance them, but that's part of the fun. As a martial arts instructor and a businessman, I found that teaching took care of all of them – one of the reasons it can be such a rewarding career. Let's look now at Freud's six needs in more detail.

Certainty

The first of the six things we all need is certainty. It is essential to have order in your life, to know that certain things will be there when you expect them to be. Knowing you will be training or teaching at certain times, for example, will allow you to plan other things around it. It is important to know that your partner or family members are there to depend on and that you will be earning a certain amount of money each year. Specifically, what makes one person feel that they have certainty and security will differ from another, but for most it is found through the avoidance of pain and unconformable situations.

Uncertainty/variety

Certainty is important but if you know exactly what's happening every day, all of the time, things will soon get boring. This is why we also need some element of uncertainty. Again, everyone's tolerance for uncertainty is different, and some people will do everything they can to avoid it. But they need it and will wonder why they aren't content. Variety is the spice of life – if you like steak and eat it every day, you will soon tire of it. Some days you'll want a burger even if it's not as good. Fighting in a competition is a great way to inject some variety and uncertainty and so is running your business.

Significance

Having something in your life that you know has significance makes you feel important and of value. This is great for your confidence and self-esteem. Significance comes in many forms. Having a special person in your life can make you feel important. Being a parent will certainly do it; and, as we all know, being a martial arts instructor and being there to support your students is another source of significance. Students can get this from gaining new belts, trophies and awards.

Connection/love

Everyone needs to feel love and connection. This can come in the form of romantic relationships, or relationships with family, friends and animals. It is ingrained into the human psyche to seek interaction and physical connection with other people. You can also feel love for and connection to a community and group, something that can be experienced through connection to your team, students or martial arts club.

Growth

It's important to feel like you are growing and advancing in life. Everything in the universe is either growing or dying. There is no in-between. You will be happiest in life when you feel like you are on course with your calling by pushing forward and learning, even if it's extremely hard work. You may feel exhausted and tired, but you will also feel content and happy as you know you are heading in the right direction.

Expanding your school and empire certainly checks this box for you, and for your team. Growth in character and confidence through training also helps to meet this need.

Contribution

Contributing and helping someone who needs it is the sixth human need. This one explains why you will often see people who have retired or already made lots of money and don't need to work anymore contributing their time or funds to charities. It feels good to help others. You don't need to give money to charity to make a contribution; contributing time and attention is just as important, and even more valuable in some cases.

Being an instructor, mentoring and contributing to a student's knowledge and character is one of the most gratifying things you can do. This is why so many martial arts instructors find it difficult to charge properly for their services as they feel they are already getting so much from the interactions. Encouraging your students to help in other classes or lower grades also allows them to experience the importance of contribution. It's for this reason that we require all students to take part in assisting classes at certain belts, and all black belts must get trained as instructors by their second Dan.

How team TopTen began

One of the most rewarding, fun, and proud times of my fighting career was being part of the TopTen UK kickboxing team. We travelled all over the UK and Europe, competing at all of the major events and winning many of them. The team was made up of a small group of some of the best fighters in the world at the time. We were elite fighters who gravitated towards each other and helped raise the bar for us all.

When my good friend Drew Neal won the WAKO World Championships in Paris in 2003, he was spotted by Peter Kruckenhauser, the owner of the world-famous brand, TopTen. At the time, Drew was training with Jason Charlesworth, who spoke with Peter about team sponsorship, and the TopTen UK team was formed.

I was training with Del Sampson at the time. Del and Jason worked together to train their fighters, so I was invited to selections. I made the original team, which comprised me, Drew Neal, Sam Timmis, Paul Busby, Jamie Wood, Nathen Markland, Dave Hughes, Lorraine Hughes, Tina Tromans and Julie Charlesworth. It was great to be part of a team again.

Together we evolved and developed, and the fighters matured and improved. The team went on to manage itself as it became more established, and we wanted to recruit some more top talent. We already had a great team but there were a few other exceptional fighters out there in the UK and we wanted to see if we could recruit a few of them.

Our new recruits were Michael Page (MVP), who went on to become a world-famous MMA fighter in Bellator, and Robbie Hughes who was, pound for pound, my favourite fighter of all time. He was ferocious, trained by world-famous Alfie Lewis at his Mushin Kais school in Liverpool. We also got Damon Sansum, who went on to fight professionally as part of the Taekwondo GB team; Owen King, who built one of the UK's biggest online martial arts teaching platforms, with some of the world's best coaches teaching various styles of martial arts (fighter training online academy); and Mieke Tate (Hink), a 6'4" woman who would kick all the male fighters in the head at some point if they sparred her long enough. These guys helped us take the team to the next level.

Standing shoulder to shoulder with these fighters was an amazing experience and raised everyone's game. When I spoke earlier about the importance of building a network, this is exactly what I meant. There is a certain mindset that top fighters have, which is not dissimilar to that of paratroopers or elite soldiers. This mindset, for a lot of the fighters in the team, carried over to success in other areas of their lives.

We also built up a TopTen UK junior team. For a couple of years, this was, in my opinion, one of the best junior teams in the world. As the fighters from the adult team retired or moved on to other disciplines, we pulled some of the junior fighters up to the adult team, along with a few others, and built a second-generation world-class adult team. This team consisted of Elijah Everill, Tom Evans, Jack Evans, Ryan Marlow, Thomas Banks, Kalon Page, Lewis Morrison, Leasha Morrison, Natasha Baldwin and Sharon Gill.

I will forever cherish the time I spent on the team, building and coaching the juniors and the next-gen adult team. Without a doubt, it helped me to develop as a fighter, coach and person.

RESTRUCTURE (REORG)

TopTen original team. Back, left to right: Tina Tromans, Jamie Wood, Paul Busby, David Hughes, Drew Neal, Nathen Markland, Sam Timmis, Lee Matthews, Lorraine Hughes. Front: coaches Jason Charlesworth and Del Sampson

TopTen winning the Austrian open team event. Left to right: Drew Neal, Owen King, Mieke Tate (Hink), Robbie Hughes, Michael Page and Lee Matthews

ELITE MARTIAL ARTS INSTRUCTOR

TopTen next generation team. Back, left to right: Lee Matthews, Thomas Banks, Ryan Marlow, Jack Evans, Lewis Morrison, Drew Neal. Front, left to right: Elijah Everill, Leasha Morrison, Kalon Page, Natasha Baldwin, Tom Evans

TopTen juniors winning the Irish Open. Front, left to right: Ryan Marlow, Elijah Everill, Tom Evans. Back: Lee and Drew

RESTRUCTURE (REORG)

TopTen juniors on the podium winning at Best Fighter in Italy 2015

Summary

In this round, we went over exactly how to restructure your school so that you can take a step back from some parts of the day-to-day to focus on business growth. For this, we used the military analogy of the 'Reorg'. We talked about what the structure should look like if you want to develop and grow your team from one person to many, and which roles you should hire first. We went over the different options for legal company structures, how to negotiate with the people you're working with and, finally, how to build a community around your school.

The next round, Round 6, is our last. We will cover how to select and train the right people to be members of your team, so you can repeat the processes from the earlier rounds and expand your empire to multiple locations.

ROUND 6
Repeat (Training And Selection)

In this last round, we are focused on how to repeat the success you've had so far. You have built a successful school and now need to plant seeds for the future and develop more instructors so that you can return to the other rounds and repeat them to build your empire. The military analogy for this round is the 'Training and selection' process.

In the military, the process of training and selecting the right people for the job is top-notch. From the selection process and throughout training, people are weeded out so that only the strongest and most suitable for the job remain.

The Parachute Regiment in which I served is known for having one of the hardest selection processes in the world outside of special forces. This is because of the type of job that you will be required to perform and the amount of stress and physical hardship it involves. If you aren't 100% competent at your job, ultimately you could get yourself or someone else killed.

After completing all of the relevant mental and physical tests to determine that you are suitable to join the Parachute Regiment, you are given a start date. At this time, you will officially be enlisted in the army and begin your seven months of training at Depot Para in Catterick Garrison.

Throughout the basic training, you are taught all of your soldiering skills along with other skills that are needed to perform the job, like first aid, map reading, leadership, team building, regimental history, fieldcraft and so on. Your physical training will get progressively harder and harder until around week sixteen, which is the official start of the build-up to the Parachute Regiment's notorious selection process, called P Company (Pre-Parachute selection). This will be physically the hardest four weeks of the recruit's life, finishing with P Company at week twenty.

P Company itself is five days long and has eight separate tests that ensure only the fittest, most determined and aggressive soldiers will pass and become part of Britain's elite. We're going to run through the P Company selection process in full, as it's what I based my black belt and instructor training on and shows the level of strength and commitment expected.

Day 1 – Wednesday

Event 1

The P Company selection process begins on day one with the 10-mile tab (a march and run with weight) over undulating terrain carrying a Bergen (backpack) weighing 35lb plus water and a rifle. This must be completed in under an hour and fifty minutes.

Event 2

In the afternoon is the 'Trainasium'. This is an aerial assault course in which the recruit's ability to react to words of command at height is put to the test.

This is a pass or fail event that includes many tests to check that the recruit can obey commands while scared and under pressure. These include an illusion jump; parallel bars over 66 feet in the air that recruits must stand and slowly walk across and then touch their toes when told to; and finishing with a Superman jump, where the recruit must run across three planks of wood at speed, jumping over the gaps and throwing themselves at the cargo net, arm first, to punch through and lock themselves in.

P Company Trainasium

Day 2 – Thursday

Event 3

The first event of day two is the log run. This is a team event with eight people on each 60kg log. It's a distance of just under 2 miles over similar terrain to the other events. This is an extremely fast-paced and difficult event where there is nowhere to hide. Recruits will also be wearing webbing and a helmet.

P Company log run

Event 4

In the afternoon, it's steeplechase. This is an individual test over a course that has numerous water obstacles finishing with an assault course. The whole 1.8-mile course must be completed in under 19 minutes.

Day 3 – Friday morning

Event 5

On day three is the 2-mile speed march. This is a fast and furious event conducted over undulating terrain. All soldiers are carrying a Bergen weighing 35lbs (plus water) along with a weapon, helmet and combat jacket. This must be completed in under 18 minutes for maximum points.

Day 4 – Monday

Event 6

After a weekend break, we have a 20-mile endurance march over severe terrain. This is conducted as a squad. Each individual carries a Bergen weighing 35lbs (plus water and food) along with their weapon. The march must be completed in under four and a half hours.

Day 5 – Tuesday

Event 7

The final day starts in the morning with the stretcher race. For this, soldiers are split into teams of sixteen, each carrying a 175lb stretcher over a distance of 5 miles. Only four soldiers at a time are allowed to carry the stretcher; the rest run alongside, ready to change over. All soldiers are wearing webbing, a helmet and a weapon.

P Company stretcher race

Event 8

Thursday's events finish with milling. This is a sixty-second no holds barred fight with another recruit of similar size. You wear 16oz boxing gloves and go toe-to-toe in full-out aggression, but there is no moving and no blocking. You must try and overwhelm your opponent with faster, stronger and more aggressive punching. You must be able to show that you are able to keep your head up and try to attack while taking incoming shots. This is about displaying controlled aggression. You must stop as soon as P Company staff say to, demonstrating the ability to turn aggression on and off on command.

P Company milling

Once all of these events are complete, the recruits attend a beret parade where they will be told whether they have passed or failed. Those who have failed march themselves away and the others receive the world-famous maroon beret.

The training I did in the Parachute Regiment along with P Company has provided the benchmark for my own black belt and instructor training courses. Our events are hard. Some of them are similar to the events I've just described, along with a scoring system to select the appropriate instructors and the best students for the black belt. In place of the maroon beret, we have the black belt and the black suit, which carries the same level of significance as the beret to those who earn it – it has real meaning and value. All BMMA instructors lead from the front – they are all incredibly fit and can fight. This means the students or trainee instructors look up to the staff and elevate their own self-image when they reach or pass the level of their coach. This is not dissimilar to the way a Para recruit looks up to their training team, and how they feel when they earn their maroon beret.

As martial arts instructors, we, like paratroopers, are in a high-performance, high-skill job. A job that teaches valuable life skills that can improve the quality of lives – and can even save them. Make sure your selection process is thorough and hard. You must be objective and make sure only the most suitable are able to get through and continue the legacy of your school. There are schools out there that just want leverage and they sacrifice their integrity to grow, by bringing in low-quality instructors just to get bigger quicker. When you build properly, maintaining quality, size will come as a side effect of your success. Let all of your students be proud of the standards and keep them high.

Training future instructors

When building a martial arts school, you will only be able to reach a certain size by yourself. To get any bigger, you must build and lead a team. From then, your level of success will be dictated by the size and quality of your team.

When I first started out, I was quite naïve and assumed everyone was like me and would do what they said they were going to do. This isn't the case. Staff training is clearly important, but even more important is the selection of the right people in the first instance – not everyone will be trainable to the level you require.

When I first started out, I trained up friends and fighters – this was a mistake. Friends are too familiar and if the business relationship breaks down then so does the friendship. It's fine if you've been working with someone for many years and you develop a strong friendship, because the relationship started out with a rank structure where you were leading and the whole relationship has developed around that, so the respect is there.

I used the fighters with the best skills as my helpers. I thought that because they loved martial arts training, they would be ideal. This isn't always the case – a lot of fighters are more interested in themselves and their own training. Some of my best coaches have been fighters, but they were selected and trained for fighting and teaching separately – the qualities required for these roles are different, and not everyone can be both.

When you start to select your SAS or SWAT team members – the pool from which you will eventually be picking your instructors – you need to make sure they are the right person for the job. The type of people you should be looking for are the ones who are doing as many classes as possible. The parents are supportive and might even train themselves. They are always early and already ask to volunteer for anything they can. If they are adults, they might already have teaching experience or experience with children.

Overall, you are after positive, happy and reliable people who are accommodating and want to help and contribute. It will soon become apparent who would be ideal when you start to look within. Think about all of your students and make a list of the top ones who would be most suitable. If you want to recruit them to your team, then simply ask to speak to them with their parents at the end of class. Most people will be flattered and happy that you have recognised their commitment.

Part of being on the team is that they get a different colour suit than everyone else. All of our beginners wear white; they then move up to blue when they go to the black belt club and are required to train more often. Our helpers, who are the bridge between instructors and students, wear red suits so that they stand out. It's important that they buy the suit and not you. It shows commitment as you have put an obstacle in the way to get in. Let them have it at a discount though. We also give them discounts on pro shop items and seminars, and you can do the same for gradings if you like. You must charge all students to get their black belt, no matter what help they are giving. Remember, your helpers are still learning and are on probation, and this is valuable mat time that will help them get to the instructor level. You should require them to help out in at least two to four classes a week, and before or after the classes they normally take themselves. It's important that they only help in classes below their level. Adults can help in children's classes, and children can help in classes at a lower belt level or age.

This is voluntary work in our schools, so you want to make it as easy as possible to fit around their schedule. As a reward, you will start training them as a potential instructor. This will entail a staff training session every six to eight weeks, where you go over various parts of this book with the team you have selected and start mentoring them on how to be a 2iC in the dojo. As they progress, they can start a full training course to become a real instructor. The idea is to plant as many good quality seeds as you can now so that in the future you have an abundance of suitable instructors. This should be an ongoing process, as you will get some drop-off.

By the time these students are black belts, they will have the required skill set as well as the right character traits to be part of your elite instructor team.

You will then be able to repeat the processes I covered earlier in this book and continue to grow and expand.

Teamwork and leadership

In order to have any real success at anything in life, you must be able to work as part of a team. Without this ability, you may be able to attain some degree of success in one area, but if you want to grow and be truly successful in multiple areas of your life, you need to learn to work with people.

Sometimes you get to choose your team; this is great as you can select only the ones who align with your values. You can build a family and train everyone in it the way that you want. When hiring for your school, you can choose your own team. Sometimes, though, you don't get to choose the team you're in. If you're around people for a certain amount of time on a repeated basis, then you are in a team environment of a sort. For example, this could be a class at school or college, a group of friends, or a sports team that you are part of but didn't create yourself.

If you are not able to work well with people, you won't be a good team player. The dynamics are different when you're on a team and if you don't adapt accordingly, there will be problems. To be successful on a team, you need to realise that the goals of the team come first. This is hard for some people to understand. A strong member of the team will pick up the slack and give more. Don't think about the fact that you are doing more than others; be proud that you are able to contribute more and help the team succeed. Look at it as an opportunity to serve something bigger than yourself.

Earlier, I mentioned the 80/20 rule; this also applies to teams. No team will have everyone contributing the same. You will get most of the contribution from a small amount of the members and the rest done by the remainder. Be in the 20% that contributes more. Be the one who adds value to everything you do, and everyone will want to work with you. If you know more about what you're doing, then mentor the other members. Encourage other stronger members to do the same. The members of the team who do this grow into leaders. Not through ego and a desire to be in charge, but through wanting to serve and help others. This type of teamwork encourages leadership – specifically, people who lead from the front and will do more for the team.

Whether you are a team member or a leader, your goal should always be to serve. Gone are the days of the boss cracking the whip from the back, unable or unwilling to do what they are getting others to do. Drive the chariot from the front. If you are a stronger member of the team or the leader, you take the hit. Do the harder work without moaning, blaming, or worrying about others not pulling their weight. The more often this type of teamwork and leadership is demonstrated, the faster others will learn how to act. You need to try and develop this mindset within your teams, so acknowledge and reward good leadership when you see it. Recognise great followers too – people underestimate their importance. In the military, there are great leaders and leadership is always encouraged, but the ability to selflessly follow and do whatever needs doing without question is equally important. The army wouldn't work without followers.

True leadership means being able to do everything and bringing everyone up to the required level by selflessly shielding and helping the weaker and less able members. If you're moaning about others not pulling their weight, then you're part of the problem, not the solution. Weaker and non-contributing members can be removed at a later stage if they aren't adding value, but people will almost always learn and improve if guided properly. When everyone is trying to think ahead and help everyone around them, it's a great feeling and anything can be achieved. If you want a strong team, you can't demand it. Be the person that you want on the team, and others will copy.

Red flags

There are certain kinds of people who make great team members and employees, but there are also certain traits or tendencies to watch out for; things that, in my experience, often suggest you'll have trouble at some point. Below are some of the red flags I look for when selecting people for my teams.

Enthusiasm without follow-through

Have you ever wanted to do something, been really excited about it, planned it, thought about it, started it and then not completed it? This habit or pattern of behaviour is common, especially in the New Year when people are planning their resolutions. Everyone is excited about what they're going to do, the body they're going to get, the new business they are going to start etc – but in most cases, it will remain just an idea.

Have you ever employed someone who was initially enthusiastic and said everything you needed to hear, started strong but then quickly died off? The same thing happens in personal relationships.

This is because when you start something new, the novelty is exciting so it's easy to feel enthusiastic and motivated. It's how we all get started on something. It's important that you have this feeling at the beginning, but it's also important to remember that this feeling won't last, no matter what it is that you are doing. You will hit a wall at some point and struggle to motivate yourself to continue; you might even stop altogether. In order to succeed, it's not just motivation and enthusiasm that are needed but drive, discipline and follow-through.

I have employed many people in the past that were super keen and said all of the right things (and were probably saying the same things to other prospective employers), but as soon as the job got tough, they dropped off. When building your team, be aware of this tendency before employing or working with someone, as people can be very convincing.

I love to work with enthusiastic and motivated people, but when I think I've found someone suitable, I like to test their resilience. The best way to do this is to place obstacles in their way, or ask them to come back once they have completed a time-consuming task. Putting a time delay on starting is another good way to see if they will persevere or are just saying what you want to hear. Enthusiasm is not always an indicator of whether someone will be successful or not; what you're looking for is perseverance and resilience.

Too nice

Another red flag to look out for is overly nice people. I'm not saying that nice people are bad team members or employees, but a lot of the problems I've had in my life have come from people who seemed nice. If someone's whole personality is based on being nice, this rings alarm bells for me. It can sometimes be the beta's way of pacifying the alphas, telling them what they want to hear to keep them onside when their intentions could be quite different.

No one is nice all the time. Of course, doing kind things for people is important, and I love to do kind things for my friends, family and business associates. But my character isn't that of a nice, accommodating and agreeable walkover. Being kind is very different to being nice. I'm motivated, fun, confident, enthusiastic, driven and kind-natured, but not nice.

If someone is agreeing to everything all of the time, they probably find it difficult to explain what they want and can quite often get railroaded into doing something they aren't happy about, without giving any indication of this. It won't be until everything comes crashing down that you find out the degree of damage that has been caused.

People like this are terrified of confrontation and never say what they really think, for fear of causing an issue. Because of this, they end up creating major problems when you find out too late.

Actions speak louder than words

Only judge people on what they have actually done. Not what they tell you they are going to do, or what their associates have done.

I meet so many people who spend all their time telling you what they are in the process of doing, and try to build their reputation based solely on this. Inevitably, the things they claim to be achieving never materialise to the degree that they have been claiming or predicting.

You are what you have already done and achieved, not what you nearly did, were going to do or were hoping for.

The 'click your fingers' test

I'm well known within my organisation for getting people to evaluate their actual position in a situation with a simple test. It's important to know exactly where you are and what you really want to do in order to move forwards in the right direction. This test is a great way of revealing this.

It is effective and simple. It's so easy to understand that I used it multiple times with my kids when they were relatively young. It's great for cutting through the bullshit and throwing reality into clear focus, and then making a decision. It shows you what *you* want, rather than what others want or what is convenient or easy. The test goes like this:

Simply ask yourself what you would wish to happen in a given situation if you could just click your fingers and make it happen.

Would you want that staff member to get in line and start being a better member of the team, or would you like them to just be gone? If you could just click your fingers and that member of staff would no longer work for you, with no confrontation, no bad feelings or guilt, would you?

Would you want to work things out with your partner, or would you prefer to be single? If you could click your fingers and your partner would be moved out of the house and you didn't have to tell them and upset them, or inform your family and friends, would you do it?

Use this test when you next experience a situation that is challenging, especially important, or both. Share your results with me on social media; I love to hear about people's experience of this test (one person I taught it to left their wife the following week – not my intention, but evidently the right decision for them).

Most of the time, we make decisions emotionally or take the path of least resistance. Are you not doing the thing because you don't want a big disagreement or fallout? In these situations, people aren't being true to their true desires and are just doing what's easiest and takes the least amount of effort, physical or and emotional.

If you could click your fingers and it be done, would you do it?

I still ask myself this question all of the time, and if the answer is yes, then I do it. No matter how difficult, awkward or uncomfortable that thing is.

This is a way to live in line with your truth rather than doing what everyone else wants you to do. It's real honesty, which is important if you want to follow your calling and be happy and successful.

Modelling success

When it comes to getting to the top, you don't need to reinvent the wheel. Find the high performers and the best coaches in your chosen industry. Hang around them, copy what they do, work and train with them, go where they go and do what they do. Who do they associate with?

I know it sounds a bit like being a stalker, but this is a recipe that works every time. I have done this myself many times in different areas, and it's what all of my top fighters who trained to be world champions did. In the context of fighting or sports, you should train with the top guys whenever you can, spar with them at every opportunity. Find out how much they train and when, and then do the same or, even better, do more.

Competition is vital if you want to be the best. When I train people, I manage their expectations and let them know that they will be fighting at least twelve times a year. This is for the ones starting out in the tournament scene. That isn't actually that much, only one fight a month. The top fighters will compete in two or more a month, sometimes every weekend. If they don't, someone else will and they will be the one winning.

In any type of tournament, you have the regulars that are competing to win. Everyone else is just filling up the draw sheet. If you turn up to an event and you're top level, you should know who your competition is and what your game plan is for when you fight them. If you don't, you are just going to be bait – someone for the good guys to warm up on.

When fighting at events, don't just fight in one section. Double or triple up. Fight in your own section, then fight in the weight, age, size or grade up. Always push up to harder, more competitive sections. Never, ever fight down. Quite often, fighters from certain clubs put students in sections they shouldn't be in, putting high grades and experienced fighters in lower sections where it's easier for them. This is the worst thing you can do. Not only because it's totally unfair for the poor kids, lower grades or light fighters getting the shit kicked out of them, but because of what it does for the mindset of the fighter who's been misplaced. They are not facing their demons; they are running from them. They know deep down that they are hiding from the hard battles. When times get hard, these types of fighters will crumble. This is not the fault of the fighter but of the coach who is making their fighters weaker. This approach breeds cowards and bullies.

The fighters who are doubling and tripling up sections and fighting guys a few kg heavier and a couple of years older or a few belts higher, will be building their foundations to become stronger, more confident and resilient fighters in the future. They need to stay on this trajectory and they will rise to the top. They are doubling or tripling the amount of competitive mat time they are getting, which accelerates their improvement.

I would put my good black belt kids who were winning their sections into the adults' black belt sections from age fourteen or fifteen, and they would often move straight up and win the section. This is because of the years spent building strong foundations.

I tell all of my new fighters that they just need to keep showing up and fighting at events, regardless of the results, and that it could take up to a year to win a trophy. It's better to manage expectations – if it's quicker than this, that's a bonus. As Woody Allen reportedly said so well, "80% of success is just showing up."

If a fighter keeps showing up, training with the top guys and fighting in all the top tournaments, then they will reach the top level as long as they have the right attitude. In my opinion, it can take around six years to become a world champion if fighters totally immerses themselves, and up to ten years for world-class consistency.

I had one young lad called Chris Aston who trained with me for over ten years. For years, he lost at tournaments. He would sometimes not even win one fight and every time would be devastated. But he kept showing up. Then, all of a sudden, he started to win. When he moved up to adults, he won everything.

I had to fight him myself a couple of times, once in a big international final. He was going for it with everything he had; I managed to get a win, but it was close and a very uncomfortable position for me to be in, a lose-lose situation. He moved on to another club because when we started to meet in the finals, he understandably found it a bit of a conflict. I retired not long after, at the age of thirty-five, and he went on to become a world champion. He is now a four-time WAKO world champion and is currently one of the most consistent heavyweight fighters in WAKO.

The losses aren't a waste of time. They help you to learn and build resilience, even though you can't see it sometimes – one day it all snaps into place, like magic.

A person's natural physical ability and physical attributes don't matter hugely. As long as they put in the hours with the correct type of training/fighting and they are committed, they will figure it out. At some point, hard-working students start to overtake the ones with great physical attributes but a half-arsed approach to training. I've seen it many times.

One of the students I trained from age four, Elijah Everill, was extremely hard-working and never missed training. His work ethic was impeccable and not only did he do all of the stuff set out for my fighting squad, he did more. Physically, there were members of the squad who had more natural ability, but they all dropped away one by one while he kept moving forward. He did all of the stuff I mentioned earlier – consistently showing up, and doubling and tripling up sections. If there was an event on, he was there. If he knew who was going to be fighting in his section, he would watch videos of them and study their technique. Anything he could do to give himself even the slightest advantage, he would do it. He was always fighting up, training and fighting with bigger, better, stronger and older students, until one day there wasn't anyone else left to fight. There was nowhere else to move up to. As a fighter and as a coach, Elijah epitomises everything I've talked about in this book. He is now arguably the most consistent fighter of his generation, with fourteen WAKO world titles to his name, twenty WAKO British titles and eight WAKO European Championships. He is the only person ever to have won WAKO British titles in points, light contact, light low kick and full contact. He won eleven open weight sections in one year, beating all black belts of all weights in the world's best events, including the notorious Irish Open in Dublin, run by WAKO World President, Roy Baker.

Elijah reached the finals of the WAKO European Championships not long after his mum passed away. Winning this event meant everything to him after losing her. Elijah's dad, Adrian, had been with him for every single fight and training session until his mum fell ill, and he was with him for this final. It was a lot to handle for anyone, but making things even worse, Elijah had the flu so badly that he could barely stand up. In a hard fight, he dug into the depths of his soul and won. He once fought an entire European championship tournament with a broken ankle. He was in immense pain. But he adjusted his style and played the hand (or ankle) he had. He collected his trophy and went straight to the hospital to have a cast put on. These are some extreme examples of what you can do if you absolutely refuse to let anything stop you.

Elijah and I opened up a school together post-Covid-19, which we named the BMMA World Champion Academy. Using the Six Rounds of Success, he has now built this into a business that runs efficiently while he is away fighting.

REPEAT (TRAINING AND SELECTION)

Lee with Elijah Everill when he gained his black belt aged ten

Lee coaching a young Elijah in between rounds

ELITE MARTIAL ARTS INSTRUCTOR

Lee, Elijah Everill and Ade Everill when Elijah won Grand Champion at the Irish Open in 2020

Elijah at his academy in Wellington, Telford – the BMMA World Champion Academy – standing amongst all of his first-place trophies

The reason people don't do the type of training I'm describing is because it's a lot of work. It takes commitment and is exceptionally hard on you, mentally and physically. You will be losing in training and competitions for a fair bit of time until it all starts to come together, and this isn't pleasant.

My job as a coach would be to move you up and put more pressure on you as soon as you started attaining a level of success. This is vital – remember, pressure creates diamonds. Unfortunately, when people start to get better at the club level, they start to drop off. But as the saying goes, 'Good is the enemy of great.' You need to keep pushing and stay as committed and as hungry as you were when you started. Don't think about how you feel at any given time – your feelings aren't important when trying to achieve at the top level.

Let everyone else have a day off or miss classes while you stay on task and keep pushing forwards. Drill and drill the basics until you get them perfect without any conscious thought. When you need them under pressure, don't build the situation into a big deal. Try and play it down as much as possible in your mind, in a 'not too bothered' approach. This will enable you to perform better in high-stress situations.

We were taught to do exactly this in the military. As soon as you come into contact under pressure, you have a condor moment (older readers will understand this) – taking just take a few moments to slow everything down in your mind before you leap into action.

This is summed up well in *Bounce*, by Matthew Syed. He quotes the famous snooker player from the '80s, Steve Davis, who said, 'Try to do the things that matter the most as if they don't matter at all,' or something along those lines.[13]

There is great wisdom in that saying as 'muscle memory', as some people refer to it, is held in the subconscious. When you think about what to do with your conscious mind, you don't tap into that subconscious (muscle) memory. Don't try so hard, just let the body do its thing – it will remember what to do when it needs to. This is why you see football players miss a penalty by miles, even when they've practised over and over – they let the pressure get to them and think about it too much.

If you want to be the player that scores the winning penalty in the World Cup final, or the one who gets the winning point for your team, you need to constantly throw yourself into stressful situations wherever they arise, when everyone else is turning the other way. Normalise the stress and, after a while, you will come to love it, to want it and to thrive off the chaos. You will then rise to the occasion.

---

13 M Syed, *Bounce: The myth of talent and the power of practice* (Fourth Estate, 2010)

Summary

In this round, we have gone over the military selection process that I went through myself, so you can understand what we use as a benchmark to ensure we get the right people for the right jobs. We also went over the type of leader you must be in order to create a culture of great leadership. We also went over the people to avoid and how to model people who are better than you at certain things in order to rise to the next level. The last part of the book will summarise what we have learned and what action steps to take next.

Conclusion

I moved to Liverpool from the Midlands seven years ago. A couple of years after I moved here, the Parachute Regiment reserves (4 Para) moved into the local army camp just 400 metres from where I live. This was a clear sign from the gods of war that I was required back one last time.

After a year or two of convincing my wife that it was a good idea, I put in my application to join. I was nearly two years over the age limit, but I appealed and they overruled it. I then went through the full enlisting process again while also training up for what lay ahead. I was rejected twice more on medical grounds, but again I appealed and it was overturned.

My application was then delayed by Covid-19 and, all in all, it took two years, but I was officially back in the army at the start of 2022, aged forty-five. I then committed myself to the hard training that I knew was coming. I had a substantial amount of re-training to do, which included eleven weekends away and a two-week camp at the Parachute Regiment's depot in Catterick. I was extremely excited to have a new challenge in my life.

I picked up a bit of an injury during my training and just couldn't shift it. I had an MRI scan and found out I had severe arthritis in my right hip from years of martial arts training, and required a new hip immediately. It was causing major problems and my dreams of being a paratrooper again were in jeopardy. I went to a specialist, who referred me to get a Durolane injection, which would help relieve the pain in my hip for a few months to allow me to continue.

Even so, I had to totally change all of the training I had planned to do. I fasted for eighteen hours a day and walked 12,000–15,000 steps daily to keep myself as light as possible. I stopped weight training and only did cardio that didn't aggravate the injury. I tried to avoid running wherever possible, unless it was required while away with the army. A couple of weeks before the last two-week camp, the injection wore off and I was in worse pain than at any time before. I could barely walk and the pain would keep me up all night. But the finish line was close, so I just had to grit my teeth and get to the end somehow.

CONCLUSION

In March 2023, at age forty-six, I was officially a fully trained paratrooper once again. It was hard, in all of the ways I didn't want it to be, but I did it. In this journey, I remembered how everything that can go wrong, will go wrong, and just kept moving forwards until I attained my goal. I'm now back in the regiment that made me the man I am today.

Lee at the end of the eleven weekends' basic training, about to start phase two. Pictured here with an old friend from 3 Para, Sergeant Major Dan Jarvie.

ELITE MARTIAL ARTS INSTRUCTOR

Lee at Depot Para Catterick after completing two weeks of phase two training with all the training team. Left to right: Corporal Donnelly, Corporal Fletcher, Corporal Foster, Lee, Captain Gaston, Corporal Daniels, Corporal Temple

Lee age forty-six after passing his re-training for the Parachute Regiment in 2023

CONCLUSION

I am still opening up new martial arts locations all the time with our rapidly expanding team. Both of my sons are now black belts, so the growth and journey continues as much now as it ever has.

In this book, I have covered the Six Rounds of Success and explained exactly how to find locations, launch your school then grow it into a successful business. We then learned the right way to go about selection and training of your staff and instructors, as well as how to set up your fight team and demand the very best from them so they can reach their full potential. Hopefully, you will have gained lessons from the experiences I've shared in this book that will help to guide and support you in your journey.

I don't claim to be anyone's guru or master. I'm just the lead scout slightly ahead of the group waving everyone in because I know the route is clear. My training company, Elite Martial Arts, allows me to offer my training courses and mentoring to instructors outside of my own franchise so that I'm now able to help more people achieve the success they deserve in their businesses and in life.

To attend one of our online or practical courses, or to be mentored by myself and our group of Elite instructors, please go to www.leematthewsofficial.com. The site also has a load of free material available, including an email course, webinar and a free consultation call from one of our team members.

Remember to think big, work hard and always look for win-win scenarios. If something can go wrong, it will go wrong – don't let that put you off. It's part of the process. Judge people on what they have done not what they say, and never celebrate until you are over the finish line. Things are never as bad as you think and they are never as good as you think, so it's always OK. Be respectful, be polite, be kind but also an absolute savage. Make yourself as hard as you physically can but don't devalue yourself by using it all the time, just use the energy, confidence and presence it gives you.

Thank you for taking the time to read this book. I sincerely hope that the information will help you.

When things get hard, smile and welcome the challenge, knowing it's part of the journey. And don't forget to say… Thank you!

CONCLUSION

Team TopTen at Bodypower with the sponsor and owner of Budoland
Back row: Kalon Page, Elijah Everill, Ryan Marlow, Natasha Baldwin.
Front row: Drew Neal, Peter Kruckenhauser, Lee Matthews.

Some of the BMMA Team at the HQ in Telford

Lee in 2003, not long after moving into his first full-time centre

CONCLUSION

A few random pictures of Lee from 2012

ELITE MARTIAL ARTS INSTRUCTOR

Doing a parachute jump is a requirement for the third Dan black belt within BMMA. Lee is pictured getting ready to jump with BMMA instructor David Gwilt (left).

Instructors Nigel Gill (left) and Toby Thompson (right) after completing their second Dan. Nigel broke his nose in the earlier rounds – that's his blood Toby is wearing on his T-shirt.

CONCLUSION

Black belt fitness test

Black belt log run in Scotland

ELITE MARTIAL ARTS INSTRUCTOR

Lee in 2023

Further Reading

Bishop, GJ, *Unf*ck Yourself: Get out of your head and into your life* (Angus King, 2017)

Cardone, G, *The 10X Rule: The only difference between success and failure* (Wiley, 2011)

Godin, S, *Linchpin: Are you indispensable?* (Penguin, 2010)

Goggins, D, *Can't Hurt Me: Master your mind and defy the odds* (Lioncrest, 2018)

Manson, M, *The Subtle Art of Not Giving a F*ck: A counterintuitive approach to living a good life* (Harper, 2016)

McRaney, D, *You Are Not So Smart: Why your memory is mostly fiction, why you have too many friends on Facebook and 46 other ways you're deluding yourself* (Oneworld Publications, 2012)

McRaven, WH, *Make Your Bed: Feel grounded and think positive in 10 simple steps* (Michael Joseph, 2017)

Noonan, R, *Bigger Isn't Always Better: A guide to corporate growth* (John Wiley & Sons, 2017)

Peters, S, *The Chimp Paradox: The mind management programme to help you achieve success, confidence and happiness* (Vermilion, 2012)

Peterson, JB, *12 Rules for Life: An antidote to chaos* (Penguin, 2019)

Robbins, A, *Awaken the Giant Within: How to take immediate control of your mental, emotional, physical and financial destiny!* (Free Press, 2017)

Sinek, S, *Leaders Eat Last: Why some teams pull together and others don't* (Penguin, 2017)

Spira, R, *Transparency of Things: Contemplating the nature of experience* (New Harbinger, 2017)

Syed, M, *Bounce: The myth of talent and the power of practice* (Fourth Estate, 2011)

Tolle, E, *The Power of Now: A guide to spiritual enlightenment* (New World Library, 1999)

Willink, J and Babin, L, *Extreme Ownership: How US Navy Seals lead and win* (St Martin's Press, 2017)

Acknowledgements

I would like to thank everyone who I have ever worked with or worked for, especially all of my instructors and teammates. In particular, I would like to thank:

My mum and dad, thank you for everything you have both done. Without your input I wouldn't be who I am today.

All of the BMMA instructors (L2 and Elite-qualified): Toby Thompson, Dave Gwilt, James McCormick, Elijah Everill, Charlotte Craighill, Tony Anderton, Ethan Kerr, Jack Buckley, Jamie Roach, Brian Fernie, Sam Jones, Gareth Brink, Jake Hughes, Mark Trafford, Bradley Matthews, Max Matthews, Zed Ahmed, Callum Jones, James Hackett, Nigel Gill, Daisy Weekes,

Steve Frost, Tom Davies, Kieren Sumner, Chloe Growcott, Kc-Mae Cooper, Harvey Polatajko, Emily Aston, Damion Sheldon and Samuel Roach.

The team at BMMA HQ: Chief Instructor James McCormick, Bradley Matthews, Mark Trafford, Lexie Cooper, Tammy Tarpey and Chloe Growcott.

The team at BMMA World Champion Academy: Elijah Everill, Adrian Everill and Jude Everill (RIP), Bradley Matthews and Harvey Polatajko.

The Kicksport team: Lexie Cooper, Daniel Cooper, Bradley Matthews, Tammy Tarpey and Chloe Growcott.

Lee, Damon and Kate Sansum, as well as the rest of the boys at Sansum Blackbelt Academy.

I'd also like to thank Tony Anderton and Emily Aston at Beyond the Battle Productions; David Lowe and Jonathan Chitwood at Budo Marketing; Jenifer Priestley at Maple Accountancy; Peter Kruckenhauser from Budoland.

TopTen, thank you for the years of support, sponsorship and friendship you have given to me and the team, and especially the coaches of the TopTen team who either coached or coached with me: Jason Charlesworth, Del Sampson, Sean Veira, Owen King, Drew Neal, Sharon Gill, Kevin Baldwin and Natasha Baldwin.

ACKNOWLEDGEMENTS

Thank you also to Gerard Turvey and the team at Nest Management, for all of the help and support you have given me over the last twenty years.

To everyone I have trained or who has trained me in any capacity, and everyone I have ever fought with, win, lose or draw. Steel sharpens steel.

Thank you to the Winsper family – Matt Winsper, James Winsper, Steve Winsper, Becky Winsper and Enid Winsper – for everything they did to help get me where I am today. You will never know the full impact you had on me.

I am grateful to Leigh Childs and John Jepson for mentoring me when I started out in business. I'm standing on the shoulders of giants.

To all the WAKO GB coaches and fighters over the years, all the WAKO national teams, President Peter Edwards and Vice President Neville Wray of WAKO GB and the World President of WAKO, Roy Baker, for driving the sport forward.

To all of the fighters, coaches and parents that are driving the length of the country week in and week out, fighting and grinding. In particular, all the fighters from Combat 32.

To all of my airborne brothers from the Parachute Regiment past, present and future. The last stand for real men, '*Utrinque paratus*' ('Ready for anything').

Thank you to all the 4 Para team who helped me get back in and through training: Sergeant Dave Walker, Sergeant Major Dan Jarvie, Captain Wisniewski, Sergeant Chris Carling, Corporal Tom Elder, Corporal Bishop, Sergeant Smith, Colour Sergeant Charlie Poore, Sergeant Major Paul Bircham, Sergeant Major Keith Sharky. Thanks also to the Parachute Regiment Depot staff: ITC Catterick, Captain Gaston, Corporal Heseltine, Corporal Donnelly, Corporal Fletcher, Corporal Foster, Corporal Daniels, Corporal Temple.

Thanks to Keian Daniels for all of the military information you provided me with, Sergeant Major Keith Sharky for the P Company pictures and Smudge Stevie Smith from SWS Fitness for the pictures and advice.

All of the TopTen UK team over the years, the originals, next generation and juniors: Drew Neal, Sam Timmis, Jamie Wood, Tina Tromans, Julie Charlesworth, Paul Busby, Lorraine Hughes, Dave Hughes, Nathen Markland, Damon Sansum, Michael (MVP) Page, Kalon Page, Robbie Hughes, Mikia Hink, Owen King, Jack Evans, Tom Evans, Thomas Banks, Lewis Morrison, Leisha Morrison, Ryan Marlow, Elijah Everill, Natasha Baldwin, Sharon Gill, Ryan Marlow, Kam Hundal, Amber Jones, Cory Cain, Cory Cooke, Grace Chandler, Paul Whetton, Marcus Ainsbury, Chloe Buck, Chloe Growcott, Asha Edwards, Dantrell Mitchell, Molly Cooper, Jack Lough, Adam

ACKNOWLEDGEMENTS

Lough, Lucy Buchanan, Ryan Hanley, Brandon Price, Kimmy Zaman, Lewis Cardin, Ben Cardin, Morgan Drayton, Finlay Ballantyne.

I am thankful also to all my fellow elite martial artists, including but not exclusive to:

The Bristol Death Squad: Sean Veira, Sharon Gill, Lloyd Allen, Phil Allen, Nathan Lewis, Lee Bailey, Stanmore Allen, Tony Cook, Sylvester Allen, Keith Allen, Jill Regan, Jason A Lemmings, Andy Cleeves, Ross Arscott, Luck Robberts, Gurj Gallon.

The American Allstars: Raymond Daniels, Jack Felton, Robbie Lavoie, Elijah Everill, Coach Hugh Smith, Kevin Walker, Willy Hicks, Regina Thompson, Joe Fife, Chris Walker, Jason Bourelly, Jadi Tention, Claire Cocoza, Chelsea Nash, Jalen Cart, Sebastien Couture, Alex Guiliani, Michael Jefferson, Leo Valdivia, Carlos Tearney, Trevor Nash, Amanda Schin, Colbey Northcutt Daniels, Sage Northcutt, Dallas Liu, Elyse Gorell, Jamal Albini, Steve Horst, Ryan Huntley.

The original SMAF team from late '90s early 2000s: Matthew Winsper, James Winsper, Mark Lester, John Jones (RIP), Robert Taylor, Linval James (RIP), Steve Leat, Gavin Sealey, Ricky Dubidat, Steve Marks, John James, Derek Smith.

The Hayashi team (my original inspiration): Roy Baker, Clifton Findlay, Mark Brown, Danny Harrison, Cory Cain, Billy Brice, Matt Winsper, Peter Edwards, Chris Collymore, Nicola Corbett.

Thanks to Alfie Lewis for his contribution to the sport as the founding father of freestyle. None of us would be where we are in our sport without standing in his footprints. I would train in my living room as a teenager to his videos. Fifteen years later we would meet on opposite sides of the mats as team TopTen UK would face his team in the finals on many occasions in explosive and exciting wars with everything on the line. Memories that will never be forgotten.

The rest of the Liverpool Freestyle/Team Mushin Kai: Marcus Lewis, Aaron Lewis (RIP), Robbie Hughes, Brendan Mitty, Steven Holmes, Ben Clarke, Lorraine Riley, Carlton Abbey, Peter O'Para, Wayne Benoni, Daryl Gallagher, Odell Kamara, Paul McBride, Mark Kelly, Tony Kelly, Carl Reynolds, Shassen Dutton, Gordon Burcham, Thomas Dodd, Simon Dodd, Callum Glover, Tyler Essam, Mike Clarke.

Team NSKA: Daz Ellis (RIP), Gaz Ellis, Bev Sturzaker, Danny Ellis, Tom Ellis, Tom Barber, Stu Quinn, Chris Nolan, Jack Swarsbrick, Ryan Greyston, Mark Watson.

Team SWAT: Peter Edwards, Clifton Findlay, Billy Brice, Chris Collymore, Lorraine Hughes, Mark

ACKNOWLEDGEMENTS

Brown, Danny Harrison, Lisa Boardman, Gemma Campbell, Terry Hillman.

ECKA, from back in the '90s: Logan Easy, Aaron Woodward, Dev Barrett, Howard Brown, Barrington (RIP), Cecil and Suger Rose, Junior Anderson, Mark Watton.

Thank you also to Greg Allison, Mark Jarvis, Craig Ward, Ryan Bratley, Simon Hundel, Bunty Hundel, Amar Dhillon, Paul Heffey, Mike Hornby, Ed Byrne, Carl Thomas and Energise, Kevin and Natasha Baldwin of Wolfpack, the Ryan sisters and family, Chris Williams, Ed Loft, Lee Thackery, Danny Walker, Leigh Charles, Bob Sykes, Tony Sykes, Deadly Dicker, Paul Gilmore, Ross Lavine, Wayne Stokes, Curtis Page (RIP), Jason O'Grady, Jason Morrison from the Bolton Dragons, Lance Manyer from TKA, Joe Tierney from Martec Martial Arts, Jamie Golding and Golding Martial Arts, Andy Cleeves, Steven Matthews, Daniel walker, Gio Marchese and all of Team Epic, Mark Junday, Matt Fiddes, Chris Boughey, Tony Dias, Alex Barrowman junior and senior, Peter Markland, Martin Bannon, Ilija Salerno, David Heffernan and Robbie McMenamy.

Thank you to all of the beta readers of the book – Damon Sansum, Keian Daniels, Lexie Cooper, Coach Sergeant Mike Chadwick and Drew Neal – your insight has been priceless, and a special thank you to Lexie Cooper for all of her help with the final edit. Last but not least thank you to all of those who wrote a foreword or praise for me and/or the book. Your words have been gratefully received.

Every interaction, good and (especially) bad, with everyone mentioned above has helped mould me into the man I am today. This book is an achievement of the collective.

The Author

Lee Matthews is an accomplished entrepreneur, coach, former paratrooper and world kickboxing champion. With over twenty-five years' experience in the martial arts industry, Lee has trained multiple world champions and opened over two hundred martial arts schools, building the UK's biggest chain of centres.

Growing up on the council estates of Telford in Shropshire, Lee overcame many challenges through martial arts training. Lee started competing in kickboxing and achieved great success – as a teenager, he won many national and international titles, and went on to represent Great Britain with the World Association of Kickboxing Organisations (WAKO) for over ten years. He went on to win British, European and world titles in multiple organisations.

Lee's determination and resilience led him to join the UK's elite Parachute Regiment, where he became a physical training instructor (PTI) for recruits and developed the mindset and outlook that would guide him through the rest of his life.

When he left the military, Lee combined his skills as a paratrooper, PTI and kickboxer to create his organisation, British Military Martial Arts (BMMA), and develop his own training courses and syllabus. Over the years, Lee has fine-tuned the processes presented in this book and has helped hundreds of instructors through his training course. Today, Lee runs multiple seven-figure businesses, drawing on his vast experience in life, leadership and top-level sports coaching to deliver training courses and mentoring through his training company, Elite. His courses give entrepreneurs and martial arts instructors the skills and mindset to succeed in business and life. Lee's passion for helping others succeed and building a community of support for entrepreneurs led him to write this book, outlining his training processes and the mindset required to succeed.

THE AUTHOR

Lee's personal story is a testament to the power of martial arts training, determination and hard work, and he continues to inspire others to achieve their goals and build successful businesses.

You can follow Lee Matthews on Facebook, Instagram and TikTok:

@leematthewsofficial